TAKING TROUT

Other books by Dave Hughes

Western Hatches (with Rick Hafele)
An Angler's Astoria
American Fly Tying Manual
Handbook of Hatches
Reading the Water
Tackle and Technique
Tactics for Trout
Strategies for Stillwater
Dry Fly Fishing
Nymph Fishing
Fly Fishing Basics
Deschutes
The Yellowstone River and Its Angling
Big Indian Creek
Wet Flies
Western Streamside Guide
Trout Flies
Essential Trout Flies
Matching Mayflies

TAKING TROUT

Good, Solid, Practical Advice
for Fly Fishing Streams
and Still Waters

Dave Hughes

STACKPOLE
BOOKS

Published by
STACKPOLE BOOKS
5067 Ritter Road
Mechanicsburg, PA 17055
www.stackpolebooks.com

Printed in the United States

10 9 8 7 6 5 4 3 2 1

First Edition

Most of the chapters of this book were written over a period of five years and published as the Fly Fishing Success column in *Fly Rod & Reel.* Those are: Reading Water, Finding Trout; Searching for Trout; The Essential Part of Presentation; Fruitful Hesitations; Bank Water; Short-Line Dry Fly; Slack Line and the Dry Fly; Subsurface Situations and Solutions; Nymphs on the Swing; Slicks in Riffled Water; Soft-Hackle Success; Fishing Stairsteps; A Half-Solved Mystery; Trout on the Bottom of the Shallows; The Portability of a Home Lake; Rod Selection for Trout Fishing; Traveling Trout Flies; Minimum Kit; Old Good Stuff; Getting it Together; Remaining Ready; The Value of Revisitation; The Angling Pace; Looking at Little Things; When a Fly Is Not What It Seems; and Insect Identification: What is a Useful Level?

The following first appeared in *Field & Stream:* Early-Season Streamer Tactics; Spike Camping for Fly Fishing; Applied Mountain Biking; and Fly Selection Simplified.

Poking at Pockets: The Upstream Approach and Poking at Pockets, the Downstream Approach were both published in *American Angler.*

Wet Flies and Wet-Fly Fishing appeared in *Fly Fisherman.*

Stillwater Strategy was translated to Japanese by editor Tomonori Higashi, and published in *Tight Loop.*

Library of Congress Cataloging-in-Publication Data
Hughes, Dave, 1945–
    Taking trout / Dave Hughes.
        p. cm.
    Includes bibliographical references (p.).
    ISBN 0-8117-2906-0
    1. Trout fishing. 2. Fly Fishing. I. Title.
SH687 .H7643 2002
799.1'757—dc21

                                                    2002020601

To the editors of the magazines for whom I wrote the articles that became the book. All are my bosses, mentors, and friends.

.The great Jim Butler at *Fly Rod & Reel*
Slaton White at *Field & Stream*
John Randolph at *Fly Fisherman*
Art Scheck at *American Angler*
Tomonori Higashi at *Tight Loop*
John Merwin, editor at *Fly Fisherman*, founder of *Fly Rod & Reel*, now Editor at Large for *Field & Stream*

Acknowledgments

I'd like to thank Les Johnson, long my friend and also editor before me of *Fly Fishing & Tying Journal,* and later manager of the GreatLodge.com Internet site. Les asked me to gather my Fly Fishing Success columns onto one disk and send them to him, and he offered to buy them for the web. Les landed on his feet, but we all know what happened to the web.

I'd like to thank Judith Schnell, my favorite editor, who on hearing about the failure of GreatLodge.com and the gathering of articles on that disk, said, "Send them to me, and I'll make a book out of them."

I'd like to thank David Detweiler, Chairman of the Board of Stackpole Inc. He accepted Judith's assignment to print the articles off that disk, read them before I did, make notes on places where they needed to be fleshed out, pared back, or torn up and thrown away, which some were. David is a fine fly fisherman and a novelist whose works evolve, at least in part, out of his love for the sport.

Contents

1

Reading Water,
Finding Trout

One of the overlooked skills in catching trout is learning to fish where they are as opposed to where they are not. Reading water to determine the most likely lies will, in truth, increase your catch more than learning to identify insects and match hatches, more even than honing your presentation skills to delicate perfection, though it feels heretical to write that.

You will rarely do well with the perfect fly on the most finesseful cast if you place it where there are no trout to take it. If you flail away with the wrong fly in the right water, on the opposite hand, placing it even awkwardly where trout have gathered, you're bound to catch a few even if it seems to be by accident.

Trout are simple folk. They have just a few key needs. The way moving water shapes itself to meet those needs dictates where in that water you will find them. The first need is shelter from a constant and pushy current. Trout are unable to stand directly in fast or even moderate flows for more than a few minutes. They need some sort of obstruction to the current, even if it's just pockets in the turbulence where water is slowed as it rushes over fair-size bottom stones.

The second key need is protection from predators. Since most attacks on trout originate from overhead, in the form of king-fishers when they're small, osprey and eagles when they attain some size, this protection can take the form of a riffled surface or deep water, through both of which birds have trouble seeing. Overhead predation is a primary reason you find trout podded up in a single deep lie surrounded by shallow water that is just as productive in terms of the things that trout eat, but offers them less protection.

Food is the third and final key factor in finding fish. The need to eat often overrides the first two needs. Trout will fight a current if some food form becomes suddenly abundant in a riffle or pushy run that has no obstruction to break the current. They will hold and feed near the surface, exposed to the stoop of a bird, if a heavy hatch rewards them for the risk they take to be up there feeding on it. They'll spend energy in a current so long as they gain more energy from what they eat. They'll sacri-fice a tithe of themselves so long as more members of the species survive because they fed on that hatch.

Whenever you explore a creek, stream, or river for trout, you'll find them where the water meets these three needs, and you'll find them absent where the water does not. In places where the water meets all three of the basic needs in generous propor-tions, you'll find a prime lie that is usually the location of the largest trout to be caught in that particular reach.

It's easy to write theoretically about reading trout water. Let me attempt to describe it in terms of an exercise that you can apply to your own actions, out where the wild waters flow. My friend Rick Hafele, coauthor of *Aquatic Insects and Their Imita-tions* and talent in the *Scientific Anglers* video *Anatomy of a Trout Stream*, has devised a little game that he plays while he's fishing in order to improve his ability to read water and find trout. I'll call it Rick's Game and condense it here.

Before Rick fishes a particular bit of water, when trout are not rising, he examines it carefully and predicts precisely where he expects trout to lie in it. Then he fishes all of the water, with-out restricting his casts to those spots. But he envisions the trout in those lies and intensifies his fishing when his fly, usually a nymph—Rick is an expert at nymphing—probes them. He is trying to confirm his predictions. The very act of intensifying his concentration where he expects to find fish might be enough to help that happen. At any rate, his predictions are confirmed often. I know because I fish with him often.

When finished fishing the bit of water, Rick pauses once again to reexamine it: to look at the water and compare his predictions to his results. Did he catch fish where he expected them to be? Did he catch other fish in lies he failed to predict? Of course, both questions are answered yes at times, no at others.

That's the game. Here is its primary benefit: Over time, as you watch the water, predict lies based on the shape of the water, then fish it to see if you're right, your expectations and your results begin to coincide more and more often. In other words, your brain, based on experience, learns to sort out clues and read the water for prospective lies more accurately. It's like life: You observe, you fish, and you learn.

I watched Rick play his game once on a broad and shallow Bighorn River riffle. We approached it together. It looked rather featureless to me, so I waded in at the lower end and began nymphing all of the water with a disciplined casting pattern—Gary Borger's shotgunning method, from his fine book *Nymphing*—as we're taught to do in water where trout could be found anywhere. I hoisted a few smallish trout and was satisfied with my minor results.

Rick surveyed the center section of the broad riffle while I fished its lower end. Then he arrowed straight to a slick in the surface that was about 15 feet long, just a couple feet wide. He fished the water leading up to the slick without any result. Then he began to probe the slick with a nymph, and instantly elevated about six nice trout into the air. All were larger than any of mine.

The reason Rick predicted them there was relatively simple, but one you'll want to remember: The slick on the rough surface was an indication to him that the bottom had fallen away. That meant there was a trench down there obstructing the current and providing depth for protection from predators, in a reach of water where the food supply all around was relatively abundant. Rick predicted a gathering of trout beneath that slick, and he was correct.

He had learned from experience while playing his game, and I learned it that day while watching him play it, that a slick in rough water indicates a trench in the bottom and pinpoints a holding lie for one or more trout. This seems such a small thing, so obvious, not news at all, but I've been able to apply it over and over in all the fishing I've done on moderate to fast water ever since: find a slick, probe it carefully, catch some fish. It has enabled me to hold quite a few trout in my hands that I would not have caught before. Now I can predict those trenches at times myself, though my predictions do not always result in trout.

But the point is not trenches; it's about learning potential lies, then proving them. The same game applies to riffle corners, boulders in runs, weed beds in spring creeks, even logs lying along the edges of lakes.

Rick's Game is fun. It's no small side benefit that you'll get to watch your own catch rate improve over time as you continue to play it.

I could try to describe the features that define potential and even prime lies—ledges, trenches, boulders, seams, edges, eddies, and others—but it would take a book, which I've already written (*Reading the Water*). You'll be ahead if you learn to read for yourself the way the water might meet the needs of the trout. When you prepare to fish any bit of water, take time to look it over carefully, think about those needs of the trout, predict precisely where the water meets them. Try to envision the trout holding, finning, feeding in their lies.

Then fish all of the water. You'll catch some trout that confirm your predictions. Those will be gratifying, and their numbers will increase. You'll also catch a lot of trout that arise from places that surprise you. These are called serendipitous; they should also gratify you.

Whenever you hook a fish, whether you predicted it or were surprised by it—whether you'd even looked at the water before you fished it—take time to examine the water where you hooked it. Ask yourself how the water met those needs of the trout. Ask yourself, "Why was that trout there?"

The critical tool in reading trout water is truly experience. It's a data bank building in your brain of what the water looked like in places where you hooked trout, and also what it looked like in places where you did not hook trout. You'll catch them most often in water that holds hints revealing that it meets the needs of trout, least often in water that looks like it fails to provide for those needs.

Playing Rick's Game, or any other that suits you better but causes you to study the water more carefully, will speed up the accumulation of data: the gathering of those bits of memory about the features of water that separate productive lies from unproductive water. Those memories, mostly of what the water looked like in the precise places where you hooked trout and therefore had some fun in the past, add up to your ability to read trout water and predict likely lies in the future.

2

Searching for Trout

On storied British chalkstream waters, anglers fish the hatch, cast only to spotted, feeding trout, get scolded if they fish blind. In the United States, from Theodore Gordon's and George LaBranch's time to this day, most time on freestone streams is spent fishing the water: casting to a likely lie with the hope that a trout will see the fly and want to whack it. I call this method *searching fishing:* finding trout and catching them at times when they're not feeding visibly on a hatch. You elevate your success at this most common method by doing all you can to distance yourself from fishing blindly.

The first thing to do when you approach a stream, whether it's new to you or one you've fished a thousand times, is to take note of a certain set of observable conditions. These will indicate what trout might be doing and tell you about the level at which they might be doing it. That gathering of clues informs you how to rig and fish for them.

The most important observable clue can sometimes be the trout themselves. If you watch the water carefully awhile, you might notice tiny sipping rises, winks of turning flanks along the bottom, or even splashy rises that are almost concealed by a riffle's dance. When you notice such activity, you've instantly elevated yourself from searching fishing to sight fishing, and you have thereby increased your chances of catching those trout.

Looking for active trout takes more than a casual glance at the water. Let me advise you of two things: Hit the stream pausing and watching rather than running and gunning, and always arrive at the stream with your rod broken down. Watching the water while you patiently string your line through the guides, check your leader, and give your floating line its daily cleaning might mean the difference between starting fishing the right way and the wrong way. Arriving unrigged means you'll more often rig right the first time for the conditions you notice while you pause and watch.

I tell you these two tips because my own habit is to hit the stream rigged and in full flight, flailing away with whatever I had tied to the tippet the last time I fished with that same rod. I don't stop fishing wrong until I'm smacked by some obvious clue that I should be doing something else. Most often the clue is that I've been fishing for an hour or more, squandering a multitude of opportunities, but haven't caught any fish yet.

If you don't notice any rising or feeding trout in your initial examination of the water you're about to fish, which is the average on freestone streams, then you're back to what I've defined as searching fishing. The next condition to observe is the shape of the water. Is it high and muddy or low and clear? Is it rimmed with ice or beaten by the hot sun? Is it boundingly swift or pooled almost to stillness?

If the water is at any of these extremes, its condition can tell you instantly how you should rig to find your fish. If the water is so cloudy that trout can't see more than scant inches, you'll know you need to thud a nymph or streamer along the bottom. If the weather is mildly warm and the water is somewhat shallow, clear, and a bit brisk, you'll know you have an excellent chance to draw trout up to a searching dry fly.

Most of the time conditions will fall short of any extreme, and you must look more closely for subtle clues as to how the weather and water might affect what trout are doing. Look for any swings away from the comfort range of trout and any variations from average conditions for the stream at the time of year you're on it. If a few cold days have dropped the water temperature from the mid-50s or low 60s to below 50 degrees F, look for the trout to be down. If a few warm days have prodded the water temperature upward, even if it's still below the same 50-degree mark, look for trout to be more active, and therefore more interested in feeding on top. If similar swings have occurred at the upper end of the comfort range of trout, a few cool days seated in a bed of hot summer days will invigorate trout, whereas a few hot days that exceed the already high average temperature will make the trout dour.

Water temperature is a clue that you can measure. If you're even mildly on the scientific side, carry a stream thermometer to take readings. If the water is 45 degrees F but it's been 35, trout might be active, but you'll probably be forced to search for them on the bottom with streamers or nymphs unless a hatch is happening. If the water temperature is 55 to 60 degrees F, that's the range in which trout have the most vigor and are most willing to burst to the surface. Try a dry. If it gets above 65, trout begin to conserve energy again. It might be wise to fish the mid-depths or to search their lies along the bottom once more, unless some other clue advises you otherwise.

After you've assessed the shape of the water and the way temperature might affect the activity of trout, look around for insects. Insect activity, or the absolute lack of it, is an observable condition that can give direction to your searching fishing. The single clue that a searching dry fly will bring you excellent success is a variety of different insect types out and active above the water. If you see gnats swirling inches over the water in a shaft of sunlight, a few random caddis in erratic flight, a sparse flight of mayfly spinners dancing over a run or pool, and an occasional awkward cranefly risking flight along the stream margins, trout notice these things, too. None of these scattered insects prompt trout into selective feeding. All of them reward the trout for an awareness about the surface. They look up. You should rig for the top. If no insects at all are out, you'll do better rigging to fish near the bottom.

Quite often the clues as to how you should rig and fish are not clearly observable or measurable or predictable, they're just something you sense. The air and water might be cooler than they've been, perhaps because you got up at dawn during a hot spell. You feel the reinvigoration of the environment of the stream. Usually you're right; trout feel it as well. Maybe you get to the stream and sense a coldness and lifelessness about it that you cannot define. You'd like to be wrong, but you're probably not. Nothing is moving, and no trout are about to be caught unless you hit them on the nose with a dead-drifted nymph. Rig to do that and you'll find fish. Rig wrong, say with a searching dry fly, and it's likely your day will be as lifeless as you sensed the stream to be when you got there.

Often intuition, rather than any particular observable condition, leads you to believe that trout are at one level of activity or another and therefore susceptible to one fishing method as opposed to another. The day might be unseasonably cool, with no insects out, yet you sense that trout will respond to a searching dry fly. You rig that way and cast awhile, and *whap!*—you're right. Why?

Fly-fishing intuition is a feeling based on an accumulation of experiences—knowledge of what has happened in your past in the same or a similar set of conditions. I'll give you a true though oversimplified example. I once waded my home stream on a drowsy day, when not much was going on. I made an idle cast with a dry fly to a shallow, flat spot I'd never bothered to fish before, just upstream from a certain rock. The sun made a circular play on the surface there and struck all the way down to the bottom, igniting nothing that made the place look as though it might be a lie. I saw no trout and expected none, or at best a tiddler. But I made the cast, and a nice trout arose out of nowhere, climbing into the sunshine and onto the fly.

Several weeks later, I fished that same reach of water in nearly the same set of conditions. When I approached that rock, I developed a sense that something was about to happen. It was intuition based on a newly experienced bit of history. I made the same cast with the same fly, spray flew again, and my hunch proved to be right.

Most times intuition—your sense of how the water and air look and feel, how to rig and fish on a certain day—is based on a more complicated set of perceptions and a much more vaguely related set of experiences than simply recall of a single cast. Perhaps you're fishing a small spring creek in southern Wisconsin, but the shape of the stream and the shape of the day remind your subconscious of an afternoon you spent on a pastoral stream in Pennsylvania. You don't register any obvious relationship or clues from your previous experience, but you do register a feeling that trout will be happy to see a size 16 Olive Beadhead nymph dangled beneath a size 14 Deer Hair Caddis, and that they might take one fly or the other but you're not sure which.

Never ignore such a feeling. Your sensitive and perhaps secret inner self, the side of you that pauses to appreciate streamside wildflowers even if the dominant part of you denies that you would deign to notice them and prompts you to tromp past them, is always busy sifting through observations and subtle clues. Anglers must tune in to that hidden half of themselves, consciously or not, far more often and more carefully than someone whose hobby is bowling or boxing. It's another reason you benefit from a brief time pausing and watching when you get to any stream: You give your inner self time to whisper to your outer self what it feels about what you see.

All of the things that you either observe or sense about water conditions, wind and weather, and what insects and the trout themselves are either doing or not doing translate into the way you rig and the way you fish the stream. In my lexicon of methods, these clues almost always lead me to rig and fish in one of four ways when it's a searching sort of day.

If I see or sense that trout will move all the way to the top, obviously I'll rig and fish a searching dry fly. If the water is somewhat smooth or fished fairly heavily, I'll usually start with a drab size 14 Deer Hair Caddis or a size 16 Parachute Adams. If the water is rough or not fished often, I'll use a bright size 12 or 14 Elk Hair Caddis or Beetle Bug—a Royal Wulff look-alike— for its greater visibility and flotation. But those are my favorite searching dry flies. You should use yours.

If clues and conditions—or just my sense of the situation— lead me to believe that trout will leave their bottom lies but won't be eager to drive all the way to the top, I'll rig to fish the mid-depths, showing them a fly a foot or two beneath the surface. The first way I'll do it is to suspend a beadhead nymph on a 2-foot tippet tied to the hook bend of a dry fly. I'll usually use a visible size 12 or 14 dry on a 4X or 5X tippet, a nymph one size smaller on a tippet one size finer.

The second way I'll rig to fish the mid-depths is with an underweighted all-fur wet fly or generic nymph on a long leader and floating line. I'll fish it down and across the current to search the water, on a slow-mended swing that sinks it 2 to 3 feet. The fly will be olive, gray, brown, or tan, all nature's colors, in size 12 to 16, nature's sizes. This is considered an outdated method, but trout haven't changed much since our fishing forefathers coaxed them, and a submerged wet fly or nymph on a slow swing has worked so often for me that I often develop an intuition that it will work once again.

If I know or sense that trout are down and dour, I begin with a split shot and strike indicator nymphing rig. I'm not sure how much the flies matter, but I'll usually use two, a size 10 or 12 Brook's Stone or Olive Scud a few inches above a size 14 or 16 Whitlock Fox Squirrel or Olive Beadhead. Those combinations, fished with upstream casts and tumbled right back along the bottom, have roughed up a lot of trout for me and are my standards. Again, you should use yours.

These are the simple keys that lead to searching success: waiting and watching, then rigging and fishing in a way that is based on what you see, what you sense, and what has worked in your own past.

3

The Essential Part of Presentation

Inserting yourself into the best position from which to cast to any rising trout or prospective lie is the key element in presentation. Your ability to assess a situation, pick the perfect place to approach a bit of water you'd like to fish, then move into that position without moving trout out of theirs can be more critical than your ability to cast 60 feet and set your fly lightly onto the water, though that ability will never reduce your chances.

Approaching the water and then wading cautiously into your chosen casting position, the starting part of your move on trout or a promising lie, covers most of the distance between you and any spotted rising trout or likely lie you've decided to fish. The cast itself is merely the delivery stroke. The more you've shortened it up, the more likely you'll set your hook into a trout, or even a bunch of them. Most of your chances for success on trout, especially those holding stations and rising steadily to insects, are determined by what you do before you ever remove your fly from its keeper and launch your first cast.

If you choose the best possible position, and move into it in the most surreptitious manner, you'll have no trouble placing your fly accurately and delicately where you want it to land. You'll have excellent control over the surface float, bottom bounce, or mid-depth swing of your dry, nymph, or wet fly. If you make the same cast from the wrong position, you'll get into more trouble with trout than trout will ever get into with you. I'll give you an embarrassing example.

Last spring, during salmonfly time on Oregon's broad and brawling Deschutes River, I fought heavy water to reach a midstream gravel bar downstream from Dr. Bub Beamer's Redsides Lodge. I achieved the safety of the gravel and was fiddling with my tackle, getting ready to fish, when a trout rose to take a salmonfly that made a fatal fall from the branches of an alder tree at the shoreline I'd just left, back across that brutal current from me. I was busy tying on a fly, and not looking in that direction, when it happened, but I had no difficulty pinpointing the take.

I once spent a season living in a hooch alongside the Mekong River, which is not a trout stream. Vietnamese soldiers on night watch nearby threw hand grenades into every island of lily pads that floated down from the Cambodian border, a preventative measure against swimming saboteurs. Delete those patches of pads, and this salmonfly rise was precisely like one of those detonations. I jerked my eyes toward the bank and saw the remnant waves of the rise washing out from under an overhanging alder limb.

The current between the gravel bar where I stood and the bank where this execution happened was too fast and deep to wade and fish at the same time. I finished tying on my fly, then splashed quickly down the edge of the gravel bar far enough to turn and launch a long cast cutting at an angle up and across the current to the protected lie of the trout.

This cast was less than easy. It had to travel 60 feet in the air. The rod had to be tilted to the right side to install a left hook at the end of the cast, in order to bend the leader around that overhanging alder and tuck the fly onto the water on the alder's upstream side, tight against the bank. I was armed with a 4-weight outfit, slightly light to turn a heavily hackled size 6 salmonfly imitation around that sharp corner.

My first thirty or so tries all fell short or failed to turn the corner, so that I either got instant drag and had to hoist the fly out of there before it frightened the trout, or got a nice drift but so far out from the bank that the trout never had a chance to notice the fly. Finally, when I was starting to tire of the exercise and was about to give up on that trout, some sort of gathering of accidents brought off the difficult cast.

The line shot across the current. The tilted loop unfurled and flicked that fly back in above the alder limb. The fly settled to the water and drifted on its bottlebrush hackles toward the scene of that recent explosive take. I became proud about my casting and braced for the inevitable detonation.

In the instant before the fly arrived where I wanted it, the swift current got ahold of the long stretch of line lying across it. It shoved a deep downstream belly into it and dragged the fly racing out of there. Water boiled up behind the fly. The trout had tried for the fly, but it couldn't catch up.

I'd finally worked out the magic for the cast. I launched it again and again. About half the time, the fly landed right where I wanted it, and I even got a drag-free drift solved by tossing an upstream mend the instant the line landed on the water. But that trout had apparently frightened itself in its one attempt at a take. It refused to rise again. Finally my bad shoulder said surrender.

I turned my back on the bank and hiked to the far side of the gravel bar, to fish for the small trout that usually nibbled at mayflies and midges that were prolific in the gentler currents there. I switched to a finer tippet and a mayfly dry and coaxed a few troutlets into taking it. I was about to begin thinking I was a fair fisherman again when I saw Doc Beamer wading out from the lodge. When he arrived at the gravel bar, he called across, "How you doing, Davie?"

"Great," I lied.

"You mind if I try along the bank over here?" Bud asked about his own water.

"Go ahead," I said. "I've worn it out."

Bud refreshed his tippet and tied on a salmonfly dry while watching the water along the bank for a while. Nothing rose over there, where I'd already put at least one trout down, but I suspect Bud knew where the trout hung out. He moved into a position on the gravel bar that was a few feet upstream, not down, from the same alder limb I'd tried to reach.

He lofted 60 feet of line gracefully, dropped it across the current, stripped slack, and tossed it onto the water beyond his rod tip. Then Bud simply held on and watched while his big boat of a fly rowed itself downstream along the bank, toward that overhanging limb, to the scene of its own destruction.

Bud's cast was trick-free. His downstream float was drag-free. Just a few minutes later, he held the results of his superior performance flapping in his hands. It was a brown trout, rare on the Deschutes River, weighing about 3 pounds.

"You can't really fish upstream to that bank from this gravel bar," Bud explained pleasantly to me while I took his photo holding that trout. "You've got to fish down to them or you get instant drag."

Doc Beamer is a better distance caster than I am, his stroke honed on years spent fishing the Deschutes River summer steelhead run. He arms himself with a rod appropriate to the big flies fished during salmonfly time, a 10-footer that propels a 6-weight line. But I could have executed his cast, even with my light rod, if I'd taken the right position in the first place. It was a lot easier cast than the one I'd attempted from my faulty position downstream from the lie of the trout.

The most important thing Bud did that I had not was to be smart enough to assess the situation and move into the best position before he launched his cast. Perhaps that's why society trusts him with a sharp scalpel and me with a dull pen.

On any river, your ability to move into the best position is often restricted by the depth and force of the currents, the shape of the streambottom, or streamside vegetation that you simply cannot thrash through. It's often possible to scout out the prime place from which to cast to a rising trout or a promising bit of trout water, but it's not always possible to get there. For example, both Bud and I would have preferred to be able to fish that alder-limb lie from the bank, but the alder tree that sponsored the limb did not allow that. We would have liked, second, to be able to wade much closer to the trout so we did not have to deliver a cast over 60 feet of currents. But the currents were so strong they denied us that access. So we were forced to cast from the gravel bar, which was our third choice. Within that choice, Bud obviously made a better selection of places to stand than I did.

Since it's not always possible to work your way into that one best casting position, you learn to prioritize positions and to take the best one you can reach without risk. Three factors help you evaluate potential positions.

The first factor in selecting a position is its distance from the rises or the lie you desire to fish with your fly. The closer you creep to where you want your fly to land, the more control you'll have over the cast and the subsequent action of your fly, whether it's a dry, nymph, wet, or streamer. If you wade 30 extra feet into a position that allows you to make a 30-foot cast to a rising trout or a prime lie, you'll be far more likely to hook up than you will if you cover the same total of 60 feet by standing back and casting long. Always get as close as you can without spooking the trout you're after.

The second factor is the current lines between the positions and the trout. These currents affect the float of your dry, the drift of your nymph, the swing of your wet or streamer. You must pay attention to them no matter what type of fly you're fishing. If the currents move in a single sheet and flow all at the same speed between a position you've taken and where your fly lands, your life is a lot simpler than if they seethe, weave, and boil around each other. When you cast over an even sheet of currents, you can achieve a drift free from drag, a swing of constant speed.

Where currents conflict, which is by far the most common condition on trout streams, you need to scout for a position that lets you place your line and leader and fly onto a single set of currents. If that is not possible, then the next best position is one that allows you to cast over the fewest conflicting currents.

The third factor, or actually set of factors, in choosing a casting position is the senses of the trout. A trout's senses are its warning whistles that a predator like you or me, an osprey or an otter, is around. The senses pertaining to position are sight, sound, and smell. Stay out of sight. If a trout can see you or the brisk waving of your fly rod, you're in the wrong position to catch it, though when trout are focused and feeding on insects, you can at times move into their range of vision if you make no abrupt movements. Don't knock rocks together when you wade into position. Don't pee in the water upstream of where you're about to fish, and don't wear sunscreen on your legs, then wade wet. Move into position in a way that honors the senses of the trout, and you're far more likely to fool them.

Sometimes attaining the best position on a somewhat smooth flat will send wading waves ahead of you, over rising trout or the likely lie you're approaching. These waves are delivered downstream by the current but don't go very far upstream against it. Wherever wading waves put you in danger of spooking trout you'd prefer to catch, move into your chosen position from downstream, so that your wading waves are carried away behind you. If that is not possible, you'll have to attain your prime position so patiently that you kick up no waves, or forget your first option and search for a second position that you can reach without bothering the trout with wading waves.

I'll give you an example of this before trotting on to a conclusion. It happened on Silver Creek, in Idaho. Jim Schollmeyer, the great angling photographer, and I were not fishing, rather just nosing around looking for something Jim could shoot with his cameras.

We spotted a fellow wading deep and fishing a circular backwater off the main spring creek. It was a beautiful setting, full of potential for action. He was surrounded by cruising and rising trout, many of them large and obviously on the feed—in other words, receptive to a fly if it happened to be the right one, presented in the right way, and in this case most importantly, from the right position.

From our own position high on the road above him, it was easy to see that the trout were catchable but he was not about to catch them. The reason was simple to see from where we sat, due to reflections off the surface of the water. He was not only surrounded by rising trout, but he was also circled by the concentric rings of his own wading waves.

From the position he'd taken, in the center of that quiet backwater and wading belly-deep in the water, the angle of light might have failed to reveal to him the cause of his own defeat. But Jim and I could see it easily. Every time he made the slightest movement to cast, a new set of rings set out to warn all those trout that danger was present. We did not stick around waiting for a photo to develop.

The gentleman's position defeated him. He could not have moved to where he was, nor raise his arm to make a cast, without frightening the fish he hoped to catch. He had disregarded the trout's sense of sight.

The wading angler was 50 feet from land in any direction. He could have more easily kneeled in the grass on shore and made his presentations from that far less disturbing position. He'd have been forced to shift his position two or three times around the edge to cover all of the water in that backwater. But he would then have been able to settle delicate casts over untroubled water, covering trout that were not aware he was around. His casts would have had a chance to connect him to a few of those feeding and therefore willing trout.

When you begin to take time to assess your options and to select the best position from which to launch your casts, you'll be surprised to discover that you're suddenly a far better caster than you ever were before.

4

Presentation to Rising Trout

Rick Hafele and I recently spent a pleasant summer afternoon casting dry flies over rainbow trout rising to midges. The stream was in a cliffed canyon of junipers and sagebrush. Its pools were 3 to 4 feet deep and a long cast across. Gentle currents ambled among scattered protruding boulders. It was a quiet, beautiful place to be.

Trout rose in steady rhythms from their sheltered lies among the boulders. They were not alarmingly selective, which was lucky for us, because Rick, a professional aquatic entomologist, collected a midge, squinted at it, and said, "It's a size 38!" He was exaggerating, but not by enough hook sizes to make it matter. Neither of us had any flies as small as those midges. We tried generic size 20 dry flies as cluster midges, and they worked.

The trout were picky about presentation, which is true about nearly every rising trout you'll ever encounter. Whenever one of us spotted a rising trout, stalked it, and got the cast and drift just right, the trout approved by tipping up for a soft, sipping take. At the sting of the hook, the rainbow would spring into the air in surprise. Few were large, but that satisfied sip and startled reaction were all we were after.

This was far from difficult fishing. With the exception of fly pattern selection, however, we were forced to solve the situation and present our flies as precisely as if those trout were the most heavily pestered and selective Bighorn River browns. Since rising trout are the grail that most folks chase as their fly-fishing experience grows and their skills are honed, understanding the elements of presentation becomes the basis for increased fly-fishing success.

The first element of presentation is almost always thought to be the cast. That's not true. It's position. Before you make your cast, you must move into the right position from which to launch it. If you choose the wrong position, the best cast will not do a lot to help you fool a rising trout. If you choose the best position, then the prescription for the correct cast nearly writes itself for you.

To choose the best position on a single rising trout or a pod of them, consider the trout to be at the hub of a bicycle wheel. Think of all the spokes of that wheel, emanating out from the hub, as possible casts you might make to the trout from out on the wheel's rim.

Your goal, given that circle with the rising trout at its center, is to select the approach that lets you move as near to the trout as you can get without spooking it, while placing as many conflicting currents behind you as possible. Scout out that one best position from a short distance, but out of casting range, before making your first move toward the trout.

Once you've attained the best position, you've solved half the problem of presenting your fly to the fish. The second half is the cast, which will be prescribed by the position you've taken in relation to the trout.

Three elemental casts solve all the problems that arise at different points around the rim of that imaginary bicycle wheel: the upstream cast, cross-stream reach cast, and downstream wiggle cast. When you've mastered these three, you'll be able to approach rising trout from any direction and catch them. If you neglect to learn any one of the three, you'll limit yourself to less than the full set of situations in which you might be able to take trout.

The upstream cast takes care of any trout you might approach from the downstream third of that circle around the trout. It has inherent advantages. Trout always hold facing into the current. When you approach them from downstream, you remain out of their sight. The current also delivers any wading waves you make downstream and away from the trout, rather than forward and over them.

In order to employ the upstream presentation, you need to learn no more than the straightforward, basic fly cast, composed of backcasts and forward casts. You can add wrinkles to it, but that basic cast, fitted to an upstream presentation, will take most of your rising trout for you, even after you've gained a good amount of experience. Everything else is built on the basic cast. Learn to execute it gracefully at what I'll call trout ranges, 25 to 45 feet, and all your other successes will arise from it.

There is, however, one critical thing to remember about making the basic fly cast to trout from downstream: If you do it on a line directly downcurrent from a rising trout, your line and leader must fly over the trout in the air, then drift downstream over it, before your fly arrives in the window where it might be seen by the trout and taken. By that time, you're lucky if the trout has not fled to Texas.

To solve this problem of lining the fish, take up your downstream position, whenever it's at all possible, on the rim of the wheel at an angle off to the side of the trout rather than straight downstream from it. Position yourself to cast cutting up and across to the trout at roughly a 30- to 60-degree angle. When you cast up and across the stream, rather than straight up, and place your fly into the feeding lane 3 to 6 feet upstream from the trout, the fish is far less likely to see the line and leader and be alarmed by them. Your chances for a take increase dramatically. If you don't get a take on the first cast, your opportunities for repeated presentations without frightening the fish also rise proportionately.

Sometimes you'll bump into trout that you can approach only from straight downstream. For example, a trout might be rising in edge currents that are too deep to allow wading out to a better angle. This is common on my home river, Oregon's formidable Deschutes, where trout feed constantly along the banks, but the water just outside of them is so deep and swift you'd be swept away at once if you dared step into it. So you're forced to present your fly straight upstream to many rising trout.

It's still necessary to avoid showing the trout the line and leader flying over their heads in the air. The situation is solved by pinpointing the lie of the trout as closely as possible, then presenting the fly tight in to it, just 1 to 2 feet upstream of its nose. Only the fly and tippet pass overhead in the air, then float back down to the trout on the water. There is less to alarm the fish.

If you fear that even your tippet might spook a fish rising in smooth currents, but you are forced by circumstances to take up your position directly downstream, you can often place your fly alongside a rising trout, and even perhaps a few inches behind it, rather than upstream from it. The cast will have to be within a foot or so of the fish in order for the fly to catch its eye. With luck, or more often with skill, the trout will then back downstream with the fly and at the same time rise up slowly to accept it. If you don't get a thrill from this sort of take, you've probably made a mistake in your choice of hobbies.

If your cast must be made somewhat close to straight upstream and your line and leader therefore will cross the trout off to the side but not very far from it, you can, with experience and some slight practice, add a curve to your cast. This will allow you to place the fly in the trout's feeding lane without the line and leader lying almost directly ahead of it.

A curve cast is not the easiest to master, and I'd recommend that you solve most of these problems by shifting your position rather than employing a tricky and at times unpredictable cast. But if you master it, the curve cast will serve you often when you're fishing from the downstream position with upstream presentations.

If you're right-handed, the left curve is executed by tilting the rod to the right on your delivery stroke, then overpowering the stroke so the loop straightens out in the air and flicks the tippet and fly around into a curve just before it all drops to the water. It sounds simple, and in truth it is. But it takes practice, doesn't always unspool just the way you planned it, and is most consistently successful when done at short range, where you've got the most control.

The right curve cast, if you're right-handed, is even more capricious and theoretical, though equally easy to make sound simple on paper. You merely tilt your rod to the right and under-power the cast, so the leader and fly drop to the water before the loop has had a chance to straighten entirely. The problem is that it's very difficult to calculate precisely how much to underpower a casting stroke so that it all comes out correctly, with the curved leader on the water at the right distance upstream from the trout, and the fly set adrift down the trout's feeding lane. If you get it wrong, you're likely to pile everything onto the head of the trout you're trying to catch. That is not a great result.

Practice these curve casts on the lawn if you can, or on the water when fishing is slow. The left curve will give you some frustration at first, and the right curve always. But in time, you'll solve situations with them that you might not without them, adding satisfaction to your fishing.

You'll find the up-and-across-stream presentation failing at times without knowing why. Everything will look perfect from your point of view, out on the rim of that wheel. Most times, when this happens, the trout is aware of some slight drag, caused by microcurrents, that is invisible from your distant position but visible from the fish's much closer point of view. You can solve this problem by making your basic cast with the rod straight up but slightly soft and underpowered. This lets the leader stack up a bit at the end.

Don't soften up the cast so much that the leader lands in a pile. Instead, take off just enough force so that the leader lands with some S-curves in it. This is not as difficult as it sounds, especially at short range. You'll be surprised, when you start making sure your leader lands loosely on all upstream casts, how many more trout you begin holding in your hands.

The upstream presentation is most useful on water that is at least slightly less than smooth. I say it that way because the flatter the water gets, the better you'll do by mastering one of the other types of presentations, but you'll often be able to catch trout on upstream casts on smooth water if your approach is cautious enough, your gear is delicate enough, and your presentation is soft enough.

The upstream presentation is usually your best choice on riffles, because the choppy water prevents trout from noticing your line in the air, though you'll still catch more if you position yourself at an angle off to the side rather than casting straight upstream. The upstream cast is fine on slightly smoother runs, so long as you can keep your line and leader from alarming the trout. When you begin fishing spring creek, tailwater, and even freestone stream flats and glides, however, you'll begin to feel the need to move out of downstream positions around the rim of that imaginary wheel, and to make the presentations these positions require, in order to fool more fussy fish.

The cross-stream reach cast is used from positions taken out to the sides of the wheel, directly across the currents to the right or left of a rising trout or pod. The major difficulty for any cast made cutting across currents is drag. This arises because the thick fly line, whether it lands lying across a single sheet of current flowing at the same speed between your position and the trout or a seething set of currents that conflict at all sorts of speeds, rides deeper in the water than the leader and catches more of the force of the current. The line is pushed downstream faster, forms a belly, and draws the leader tight. The fly begins to scoot, trailing a wake, turning trout away. If you make a cast straight across currents, in the best situation you'll get just 2 to 3 feet of free drift before you get drag.

The reach cast, detailed in Doug Swisher and Carl Richards's book *Fly Fishing Strategy,* solves this drag problem. It's an especially effective presentation method when you're casting to a pod of feeding trout on smooth water. It allows you to extend the free drift of a dry fly by several feet on a cross-stream cast and to present your fly to a single rising trout without fear of lining it. The reach cast gives you an extended drift, showing your fly attractively to more than one trout if you're lucky enough to get into a pod of them.

It's always best to single out a trout and aim your cast specifically to it, no matter how big and dense a flock of them is rising all around you. But you'll always gain an advantage, which translates into extra trout held in your hands, if other trout get a chance at your fly after the targeted fish has for some foolish reason let it get by.

The best position from which to make a reach cast presentation is at a slight angle upstream from the trout. This slightly reduces the angle of purchase the current has on your line and retards drag a few seconds, which adds feet to your free float. A position directly across the currents is almost as good, but you'll get just a bit shorter float. The reach cast is also effective when you take a position a bit downstream from straight across, but as you move more to an angle below the fish, you increase the chance that it will observe the line in the air on the cast.

This cast is designed for presentations to selective rising trout on smooth water. In such situations, trout tend to be more wary than they are in rougher water, because they are more exposed to overhead predation by kingfishers and osprey. They are also able to see better through the smooth interface between water and air. Any news given to the trout about the arrival of your line, leader, and fly is likely to spook it on this kind of water, so you must do everything you can to reduce that chance.

To execute the reach cast, measure the distance to the rising fish or the one you've singled out in a pod of them with normal forward and backcasts. Tilt these measuring casts off to the side. If you aim them straight at the trout, you know what will happen. Strip a few feet of extra line off the reel, then aim your delivery stroke precisely to the point where you want the fly to land. While the line loop of the delivery stroke unfurls in the air, tip your rod over upstream and reach upstream with your rod and arm. If you're after the maximum amount of free drift, lean upstream with your body and reach out as far as you can. Let that extra line slip through the guides as the cast arrows out toward the lie of the trout, compensating for all this tilt and reach.

Your fly will land right where you aimed it. Your line will follow the rod tip and land on the water at an angle downstream to the fly, rather than cutting straight across the currents from your position. As the line, leader, and fly all drift downstream, the line will travel behind the leader, slowly catching up with it, rather than quickly forming a belly and causing consequent drag.

Follow the drift of the fly downstream with your rod tip, and you prevent a tight line from forming. Your fly drifts freely down the trout's feeding lane or several feet through a pod of rising fish.

To extend this free drift, follow with the rod until the line is straight from you to the fly and the rod is pointed straight down the line. As the drift continues, reach across in front of your body, and extend your arm and the rod to follow the fly downstream from your position. This will let the fly drift freely for as far as

20 feet on an even sheet of current, though 5 to 10 feet is a more likely outcome on a set of seething currents. That's several times the free drift you'd get if you made a cast straight across the same set of currents. If you want a longer float, lean your body over as well, but I'm not liable if you tip so far that you fall in.

The reach cast is a lot easier to execute than either of the curve casts described above. Condensed, you do no more than aim your cast, tilt your rod, and reach while your line flies out, then follow the fly with your rod tip after the fly has landed. That's all.

Your compensation for learning this reach cast, and using it in smooth-water situations where the best position is out to one side of the trout, will at times be three to four times the number of trout hooked. That ought to be enough. But there's an added benefit that will manifest when you begin applying the method on water.

It's simply this: When you begin working with this cast, you'll find yourself first moving in closer to the trout so you can execute it more accurately. Because you've moved in closer to the trout, you'll make slower movements, tilt your rod out of sight of the trout, cast more accurately, and place your fly onto the water more delicately. All of these are important aspects of fishing to rises on smooth water. They're very important in the reach cast, but you can use them in upstream presentations and the next presentation method as well.

The downstream wiggle cast solves problems arising from an approach and position taken in an arc upstream from a rising trout. The primary advantage of such a position is great: The fly is always delivered to the trout ahead of the alarming line and leader. The fly is the first thing to arrive in the trout's window of vision, and it arrives as if unattached to anything, just as a natural insect might.

The problem with any normal cast from anywhere upstream from a trout is obvious: You get a tight line and instant drag. To solve this, you must introduce slack into the line and leader when they land on the water. As this slack feeds out, the fly is given a drag-free ride right to the trout. Mel Krieger's downstream wiggle cast introduces this slack and is detailed in his book *The Essence of Flycasting*.

The best position for the wiggle cast, around the rim of that wheel, is upstream from the trout but off at an angle that can be slight but not straight upstream, around to the side so far that this cast merges into a reach cast. Adding some creative wiggle to a reach cast can make it more effective. In most circumstances, your position for the wiggle cast will call for a cast at an angle of around 30 to 60 degrees downstream to the trout you've singled out.

With the wiggle cast, you'll never get an extremely long drift, and you're always better off casting to a pinpointed trout than to a pod. Once the slack goes out of the cast, the line, leader, and fly will all drag across the water. It's easy to steer the whole affair away from a trout so that this drag takes place out of its sight. If you try to fish a dry through even a small pod of trout, however, your retrieval for the next cast will almost certainly spook the entire outfit. Single out a trout, and if it's rising in a pod, make sure it's one that is off to one side or the other of the rest of them.

If you find yourself in the rare desperate position of needing to cast directly downstream to a trout, the wiggle cast will solve your problem, but it will give you only one good drift over the fish. The fly will float to it ahead of the line and leader on that one cast but will also follow it over the fish if you get a refusal. If a way to lift it off the water without alerting the trout has been invented, I haven't heard about it. You get one shot at it. Avoid a position directly upstream from a trout if at all possible.

To make the wiggle cast from a preferred position upstream and at least to a slight angle off to one side or the other of the trout, begin with basic casts, tilted off to the side so the trout cannot see the line in the air, to measure the distance to its feeding lane. Work a few feet of extra line beyond the rod tip, and carry it in the air. Aim your delivery stroke right at the feeding lane and 2 to 6 feet upstream from the trout. Usually closer is far better, because a longer float gives currents time to remove slack from the leader and embed invisible microdrag in your drift.

As the line loop unfurls on the delivery stroke, briskly wiggle your rod tip back and forth. This will cause the line to land on the water in a series of S-curves.

If you wiggle your rod as soon as power is taken off the delivery stroke and the line loop begins to unroll in the air, the S-curves will land in the leader and the distal end of the line. This is generally the preferred outcome, since slack near the fly serves to give it a free float, and slack back away from it gives the entire leader and front end of the line a free drift but doesn't do anything about microdrag.

If you wait a beat or two while the line begins to unfurl and wiggle your rod after the loop has formed, the S-curves will land farther back beneath the rod tip. If you wiggle the rod the entire time the line is in the air, you'll have S-curves from fly to rod tip. By adjusting your timing and by practicing enough, you can learn to lay slack into your cast anywhere you want it, from rod tip out to the business end of things.

Such a fine amount of control will serve you well in a few fishing situations, but in truth, it will be most useful in impressing your friends. Most often, you'll want slack out near the fly, especially in the leader and tippet, to give the fly maximum free float.

If you desire to extend the drift from the back end of the operation, the best way to do it is to strip extra line off the reel and toss it onto the water just beyond the rod tip. You should master this, as you'll find it a very useful technique to reach rising trout that are coming up over deep water downstream, where you cannot wade and can reach them only by feeding lots of slack into the back end of your drift.

I've often been asked, as I've spoken at fly-fishing club meetings around the country, what I consider the one critical skill that would most increase the catch in fishing to rising trout. My answer is the wiggle cast. I can't count the times that I've worked over feeding fish from downstream, failed to catch them no matter how many times I changed flies to match the naturals, then moved into position to cast downstream to the same fish and fooled them with nearly any of the flies they'd refused with such disdain.

The wiggle cast is more difficult to master than anything but a curve cast. The reason lies in the amount of line taken up by the S-curves. It's easy to measure the distance to a trout's feeding lane on a straight cast but harder to calculate how much extra line the wiggles will require. The only answer is not to calculate, but to gain experience and let your arm and eye do the math. You'll be surprised how quickly your body is able to figure things out without cerebral interference.

I'd like to insert a brief but critical review of rods for presentation fishing at this point, one that will be expanded upon later in the book. The wrong rod will possibly cause you some problems but won't defeat you in the upstream cast and cross-stream reach cast. But the wrong rod can make a wiggle cast impossible. If your rod is too stiff to wobble at the tip, which is true for a disappointing number of distance tools on the market today, you won't be able to create S-curves. If your rod is so soft that it wobbles all the way down in the butt rather than out in the upper end, you'll never be able to create the 1- to 3-foot S-curves that you'd like to have land on the water. Your S-curves will be few and about 10 to 15 feet across, of no use to you in any sort of trout fishing.

Rods that work best fall in the broad range that would have been called fast action twenty years ago, before fast came to mean a rod that wouldn't bend until 60 feet of line were in the air. Ideally, you need a rod that flexes out toward the front on a short cast, then works down closer toward the butt as you increase the load on it. Such a rod will respond to the impulses of your wiggles and install the narrow S-curves you'd like to see on the water.

The object of each of these three presentation casts—upstream, reach, and wiggle—is to increase your chances of fooling the trout. Each improves your odds by giving you a drag-free drift over rising fish no matter which position you take for the cast: above, out to the sides, or below the lie. Each also improves your odds by giving you chance after chance at the same trout without alarming it.

You'll use one of these three casts most of the time in fishing over rising trout. The one you choose will usually be dictated by the position you take around the periphery of the trout. But you should never consider yourself restricted to any of the casts. Many times, you'll catch more fish if you construct what I'll finish up by calling creative casts. These are combinations of the basic presentation casts.

As an example that I've already mentioned, the reach cast can nearly always be improved upon by adding an element of wiggle on the delivery stroke. It's not that hard; just wiggle the rod tip as soon as you lay it over into the reach. This results in slack in the leader and a much better drift. Another example would be adding some wiggle to an upstream cast when you're fishing over smooth currents but can't wade into position for a reach or wiggle cast. Even on a riffle that is bouncy but also heavily fished, I've seen times when some wiggle added to any cast would add trout to the catch.

A final example would be some elements of reach added to a downstream wiggle cast made from off at a sharp angle to the trout. But this shades into a debate: Is this a cross-stream reach cast with wiggle added or a downstream wiggle cast with reach added?

You get the picture. Go create your own casts.

5

Fruitful Hesitations

If you're like me, the instant you spot a trout rise, you move into position to cast to it and fire away with whatever fly you've already got tied to your leader. Sometimes that works, especially if you're in the midst of a hatch and you've worked out on other trout an imitation for what you know that trout is taking. If you've just arrived at a new bit of water, however, or you've been fishing for a while but the trout have just started to rise, that hasty cast has more chance of failure than success.

A few moments' pause between the first spot and the first cast will greatly increase the chances that the trout will respond to your first cast, which means you won't put it down. It also increases the odds that other trout will accept your fly on subsequent casts if you take a bit of time to figure out how to catch the first one.

The first hesitation, between spotting a rise and casting to it, should be for a minor amount of observation. Watch for a second rise in order to locate more exactly the position of the trout's lie and therefore calculate more carefully where you'd like your fly to touch down on the water. But that's not the most beneficial result of taking a moment to watch for a second rise. The most important thing is to notice the level at which the trout is feeding.

When you see a rise, it's easy to assume that a floating adult insect has gone down to death, especially if you see mayfly duns, caddis, or stonefly adults in the air or on the water. A surface take is always the highest probability, but there are others, and they need to be considered. Trout sip mayfly emergers from the film and take rising nymphs just beneath it. They chase caddis pupae and intercept them just before they reach the top. They even take some stonefly nymphs, notably yellow sallies, just as they approach the top to emerge out in open water, where stoneflies are never supposed to hatch.

All of these trout activities create visible riseforms. When you see a rise, you need to run all of them through your head, weigh them against the chance that the trout is feeding on the surface or just beneath it. If it's feeding on top, then your normal calculations and a dry fly will usually catch the trout for you. For the rest of that high percentage of the time, when the trout is feeding subsurface, if you fail to notice it, you'll catch little but aggravation on a dry fly.

The form of the rise, once you take time to observe it, will tell you when and how a trout is feeding. If you see the nose of the trout break the surface, or if a bubble is left in the rise, it took something from the film. If you don't see a nose or a bubble, even if you do see the trout's tail follow and break the surface, at least suspect that the take is to an emerger, or to a nymph or pupa so close to the surface that the rise rings break through to the top. If you're in a riffle and see trout rise with a spurt of water, what the great Gary LaFontaine calls a pyramid rise, in the choppy water, suspect that the trout has taken a rising mayfly nymph or caddis pupa even when you see adults of the same insects on the water.

The key is observation. Once you've opened your eyes and mind to possibilities other than surface takes, you'll be surprised how often you notice that a rising trout is taking some other stage of an insect when you thought it obvious that it was feeding on adults. That information translates into the fly style from which you need to select an individual dressing to imitate what you now suspect the trout is taking. I'll give you a quick example, which will deliver us to the next set of important hesitations.

I once fished out a productive bit of bank water on my home Deschutes River, caught a satisfying number of trout, got back in my drift boat, and bounced downstream just a short distance to a riffle. As soon as I pulled the boat to shore below the riffle and waded back up to it, I noticed spurting rises in the seam down the length of the edge of the riffle. Caddis adults bounded about in the air just above the water. I'd been using a Deer Hair Caddis with pleasant results along the bank I'd just left upstream. I hopped out, waded in, and began to cast it, but I didn't even get the honor of any refusals. That's when I inserted that first hesitation, to check my assumptions about the level at which those rising trout fed.

I noticed then that few of those adult caddis in the air ever touched down to the water, and none that did disappeared in rises. I understood—empirically, for there was no evidence but my own experience—that the trout must be intercepting caddis pupae on their way up for emergence. I clipped off the dry fly, tied on a LaFontaine Olive Sparkle Pupa about the size of the adults, fished it on the swing over the rises, and at once began to entertain a few of those trout.

That second hesitation, after taking time to notice that the trout were not taking adults, was directed toward determining which new fly to tie to my leader to replace the failed dry fly. This thoughtful pause was broken into two parts, the first for choosing a fly style, the Sparkle Pupa, the next for deciding which precise pattern to use within that style.

When trout feed on the surface itself, selecting a fly style and dressing can be easy, because you can observe directly what the trout are taking. Catch a natural in your hand or suspend the aquarium net that I advise you always to carry in the surface film and intercept a natural adult from those boating by. Choose a dry fly the same size, shape, and color. Let's not dwell on that.

When trout feed subsurface and you've chosen to go to a sunk-fly style, it's more difficult to collect evidence on which to base your choice of the right individual dressing. Sometimes you can suspend a net and capture a living beast on which to base your choice. More often you need to make an educated guess. The education for this guess can come from experience, which is the most enjoyable way to acquire it, as it requires extensive time spent fishing, or from research and reading the fly-fishing literature.

A bit of time spent thumbing through hatch-matching guides will reveal to you what the stage preceding the winged adult looks like for whatever aquatic insect might be in the air or on the water in front of you. By this I mean that with a little fore-knowledge, capturing little olive mayfly duns *(Baetis)* will tell you to fish a Pheasant Tail Nymph for the emerger, observing spotted sedge caddis adults *(Hydropsyche)* is an indication that an Olive Sparkle Pupa will work for the pupae, and collecting yellow sally stonefly adults *(Isogenus* or *Isoperla)* will instruct you to tie on something as simple as a Light Cahill wet fly. Base the size of the fly you choose on the size of the adult insect you collect.

That is a far reach from covering all of the possibilities that you might encounter in that second hesitation, in which you often must select a sunk fly to match the immature stage of whatever adults you observe on the surface. But it gives you an idea of how such associations are made. You'll have to acquire that experience—sorry, it's an assignment to go fishing a lot—or do the rest of that reading yourself.

At the end of this second hesitation, you've now noticed which stage of what insect the trout are taking and have armed yourself with not only a fly in the right style, but an individual dressing within the style to match it. You have not just matched the hatch, but the stage of the hatch on which your trout is feeding. Just one slight hesitation is left before the cast: You must check your rigging to be sure you can fish that chosen fly right.

Most of the time, this means no more than nipping off the dry fly you've been using and tying on whatever fly you've chosen to replace it. The subject here is a spotted, visible rise. Even if you're going to fish a nymph or wet fly, you're not going to rig with a split shot and strike indicator, because an observed rise never involves a trout feeding along the bottom. Any changes you make to your terminal tackle, if any at all, are bound to be simple.

The most common change necessary is to add some length to your tippet. Whenever you get into a selective situation, and trout refuse what you're using, always inspect your tippet before making any other change. You'll be surprised how often it has contracted, through constant fly changes, to about a foot long. Extend the tippet to 2 to 3 feet and you can often bring back business without even changing flies.

If you're changing from a dry fly to fish a sunk fly, whether an emerger, nymph, or wet, you'll find times when it helps to make a final change. I'll illustrate it by getting back to that riffle on the Deschutes, where adult caddis were in the air but trout refused to take drys. The trout were taking caddis pupae on their way up for emergence. I took that as an indication for the Olive Sparkle Pupa. I knew the trout weren't seeing the natural caddis pupae swimming swiftly, but rather swimming feebly and being buoyed to the surface by gases trapped under their outer cuticles. Trout wouldn't be eager to take the fly on the gallop. So I added 3 feet of 5X tippet to my leader, then tied a small, yellow yarn indicator about 5 feet up the leader from the fly.

I took my position off to one side of the rising trout and presented the Sparkle Pupa with cross-stream reach casts that let it amble idly along with the current. That's when trout began to accept it.

This entire set of hesitations—one to puzzle out whether trout are feeding on the surface or beneath it but sending rises up to the top, a second to decide on a pattern style and within that a specific dressing, and a third to rig right to fish the chosen fly—might sound complex but will take on average just two to three minutes on the water when you spot a rise. If you practice a bit of patience and add those slight steps between the instant you spot a rise and the moment you begin casting to it, you'll more than double your chances of success over it.

Once you've found the solution for that first fish, others are sure to get in line to whack the fly you've chosen.

6

Bank Water

When I began fishing bank water for trout in my youth, I thought bank fishing meant standing on the streambank and casting from there to whatever water I could reach. I was able to cast only 20 to 30 feet. I rose a few trout in that relatively barren zone near but not next to the banks and thought that was doing quite well. The water beneath my feet and flailing rod tip remained neglected. I knew no trout would hold so near to the danger I mistakenly perceived myself to be.

A long time later, I learned that whenever I fished the banks that way, I was no danger except to my own chances of catching trout. I was, in fact, a large object in dire need of removal. Once I stopped thrashing right up to the edge and waving my rod around over their heads, I discovered that most trout that choose their lies in relationship to the edge hold a few inches to a foot or two, rather than a few feet, away from streambanks.

Now I know that bank fishing means creeping low and slowly among grasses, willows, alders, poison oak, and rattle-snakes, keeping myself and my rod out of sight, casting the same

20 to 30 feet, but upstream and tight to shore, no more than 2 to 3 feet out. If I see a feature 5 to 10 feet out, perhaps a boulder breaking the current or a seam where two currents come together, I probe that water carefully but don't consider it to be bank fishing when I do. Bank water is the narrow strip of water where the current is modified by the way it flows along the edge.

The banks of any stream are the transition line between the aquatic and terrestrial environments. Stonefly and some mayfly nymphs, plus a scattering of caddis as either larvae or later pupae, migrate from midwater to shore in order to climb out for emergence. Grasshoppers, beetles, ants, and crickets drop in from the landward direction. Trout gather at the banks waiting for all those groceries to arrive by sea or by land.

Trout do not move to lies along banks until some food form arrives to attract them there. Most folks think only terrestrials entice trout to the banks and confine their bank fishing to late summer and early autumn. Trout are there then. But on many streams and rivers, they move to the banks a lot earlier, in some cases as soon as runoff has calmed at least a little. On my home river, the Deschutes in Oregon, trout follow the migration of salmonfly nymphs to shore in late May. They remain on the banks, well fed, until terrestrials begin to wither in the first cold of late fall. Salmonflies migrate to shore on Montana's Madison River in June, and trout can be found there the rest of the long season. On the Yellowstone River, the same thing happens, but usually a few weeks later, in July.

Every stream will have different timing, but each will be fairly consistent from year to year, within consistent weather conditions and water levels. The arrival of trout along the banks might be early or late in the season, but it will usually be triggered by some observable food form, whether aquatic or terrestrial. Learn to recognize it, and you'll learn when it's time to turn your attention to the banks each season on your own home waters.

Next you need to learn to pinpoint trout lies along banks. In the average stream, just 10 to 20 percent of the bank water is worth fishing. You can neglect the rest and not pass up many trout.

Some streams have little good bank water, others much more. Waters subject to spate and then subsequent low flows have the least good bank water because their banks are eroded during high water, have little slope, and therefore little depth along the edges when the water recedes. Streams with stabilized flows, such as spring creeks and tailwaters, suffer less erosion and therefore have steeper banks, with more depth at the edges at low-flow periods, when it's most likely food will attract trout to the banks and you'd like to fish for them there. Stable streams will therefore have a higher percentage of good bank water than spate streams.

Three factors define good bank water, and to be good bank water, it must have all three, not just one or two. The first is at least a modest current to deliver food. Bank water that lacks current generally lacks trout, or at least those of much size, because they'd go hungry holding there.

The second factor is some depth or cover to conceal trout from overhead predators. If the water drops almost straight off to a depth of 2 or 3 feet, trout will hold there. If it slopes off so slowly that it is 1 or 2 feet deep 5 or 6 feet away from shore, trout might hold farther out, but not in the thin water near the bank unless an overhanging limb or bunchgrass clump offers them something to hide beneath.

The third factor defining fishable bank water is some obstruction to the steady flow of the same current that delivers food. If you find boulders on the bottom, indentations in the shoreline, or logs, limbs, and roots to break the current, you'll find trout. If the current sweeps the bank like a broom, trout cannot hold there because they are not strong enough to swim constantly against a steady current, even a modest one.

You find good bank water wherever the three factors converge: current next to the bank, depth or some sort of hiding cover right next to it, and some obstruction to break the current. Scout the banks until you locate a lie, or more likely a short or even long reach of prospective lies, with all three indicators gathered together, and you've found trout. You're ready to rig to fish the banks.

When gearing up for bank fishing, you're again after three things: control, control, and control. First, you must have control over the line in the air because of the restricted environment you're in along banks. You'll have tall grass, shrubs, or sagebrush all around you. If you don't have limbs and trees interfer-

ing in your backcast area, you don't fish the same kind of banks
I do. In order to fish bank water well, you need to be an adept
rod and line handler to avoid all the obstructions to your casts.

Second, you need at least adequate control over where your
fly will land. If you can't hit your hat on occasion at 20 to 30 feet,
you aren't going to place your fly into enough of those small
pockets of convergence to harvest much more than frustration.
If your usual practice session or average fishing excursion consists of seeing how far you can cast, take a few minutes each
time you're out, either practice casting or fishing, to work on
precise placement at close range, some of it while casting from
your knees.

The third kind of control you need is over the drift of your
fly once it lands on the water. If you fail to get at least 2 to 3 feet
of drag-free float, you're likely to put more trout down than
you draw up. You achieve control over the float by creeping as
close to a bank lie as you can to reduce the number of conflicting
currents between you and the lie, by rigging with a leader the
length of the rod and a tippet at least 2 feet long and fairly supple
for the size fly you're fishing, and by dressing the leader with
floatant to within a foot of the tippet knot. The leader will then
skate. All those conflicting currents you cannot get behind you
will get less grip on the leader and not tug your fly around so
disastrously.

To achieve these three kinds of control, you need a balanced
outfit: rod, line, and leader. The rod should be 8 to 9 feet long,
light, bossy, and with an action that could be called a bit quick,
for tight loops and maximum accuracy. The line should be a
floater, double-taper or weight-forward, your choice, but heavy
enough to load the rod on a short cast. If you have trouble with
control on short casts, the first thing you should try is a line one
weight heavier on the rod you already own. You might discover
that a cranky rod is suddenly sweet for poking flies at bank
water.

Fly choice along the banks is slightly more restricted than
when you match hatches over selective trout. I used to fish nothing but Elk or Deer Hair Caddis at the banks. I still use those,
but I pay more attention now to any natural insects around, in
the air or on streamside vegetation, and try to match them at
least roughly. If nothing is predominant, I still use those old

searching dressings, but in sizes 14 and 16 where I used to use them in sizes 10 and 12. That drop in dry-fly size often creates a surprising increase in the catch, along banks or anywhere else.

Don't drop down in size if grasshoppers or salmonflies are in even minor abundance at the edges. If you see any big bugs at all along the banks, imitate them and hold on. If you see ants, on the opposite hand, or tiny beetles, refine your tackle, lengthen your tippet, and prepare to make some of the softest hook sets.

Dry flies solve bank situations most often because trout see most of their food flop down from overhead. But you'll often goose your chances at bank trout if you drop a small nymph off the hook bend of your dry fly on a 20-inch tippet of 5X or 6X. Be sure you don't sacrifice control over your casting to add a dropper. If you can no longer hit small targets and get drag-free drifts, nip off the nymph or replace the dry fly with a tiny indicator.

I fish the banks more and more often with a size 14 or 16 beadhead nymph below a small yarn indicator 3 to 5 feet up the leader. This works especially well on gentle meadow or tailwater streams with grass banks and undercuts. The nymph dangles down just deep enough to be seen by trout holding back out of sight and sheltered from the passing current. They'll dash out. The indicator will duck under. That's as exciting as a take to a dry fly, at least to me.

The largest modification in my own bank fishing has been the speed at which I propel myself. I used to trot right along, covering a mile or more of bank water in an average day. The more bank water I saw, I calculated, the more trout I'd catch. Now I spend time waiting and watching each bit of bank water I approach before I ever fish it. It might take me half a day to fish a couple hundred yards. At the end, I'll have held more trout and be faced with a shorter hike back to the rig.

I read the water carefully for the three converging factors that make it a likely bank lie: current, depth, and obstructions. Then I watch for trout to expose themselves with rises, winks underwater, or swirls at the surface indicating takes just beneath it. These things reveal the trout and also what they might be willing to accept in the way of a fly.

Once you've found trout and figure out what fly they'd like, you can pluck them like berries along the banks.

7

Short-Line Dry Fly

I spent a few fall days fishing Colorado's Frying Pan River a couple seasons ago with Ed Engle, A. K. Best, Mike Clark, and John Gierach at Roy Palm's place. The philosophy and fun around the campfire at night were at once as enlightening and as puzzling as the great John makes them out to be in his beautiful string of books that began with *Trout Bum*, which is where I'd recommend you begin to read this author who has defined, more than any other writer, our angling generation.

One early afternoon, we were sprinkled up and down the river. John was off in a corner pocket, casting at a large, lofting nose. Ed waded powerfully across to fish the streamy currents on the far side. A. K. patiently pestered a trout that set up a rise rhythm, feeding on something tiny, on a long, smooth flat. Mike, whose fine bamboo rods all of those other characters cast, was somewhere out of sight, educating trout all by himself.

I discovered myself centered in a broad and fast stretch of currents that bounded 2 to 3 feet deep down a boulder-garden run. I fished a dry fly and did far from well until I suddenly realized I'd failed to adjust my fishing to the water in which I found myself. I was too busy watching those other guys, all lofting long-looped and graceful casts that worked on the water where they were. It was pretty to watch them, and I fell into the mistake of casting a long line myself.

I don't always do well in short-line situations because I like—I almost demand—that the grace of fly casting be an elemental part of my fishing. I don't mind fishing with rough, almost ugly flies, in part because that's the kind I tie best—I'm always in a hurry to tie a few so I can get back onto the water— but also in part because the insects our flies imitate are themselves usually roughed up by water before they're taken by trout. I do believe that the delivery of those awkward assemblages should be graceful, because I see the grace of the fly cast to be very near the center of the definition of fly fishing.

Catching fish on flies, however, is the center itself, so I unsheathed my Folstaf, leaned on it with my left hand, and began casting no more than the amount of line I could easily control, both in the air and on the water, with my right hand and the line clamped tight. That amounted to just the leader and a little over a rod length of line.

Within half an hour, I was totally into my own fishing, my focus drawn from those other graceful fellows to my own brutal stretch of water by the simple fact that I was suddenly extracting out of it a fair portion of fat trout. I found myself enjoying even the casting, for there were ways in which I was forced to amend it to fit the situation, and not all of them lacked grace.

Short-lining a dry fly in fast water increases your odds— almost logarithmically in proportion to the amount of line you rein in—for several reasons. You can read the water and spot those microlies that are the true secret to extracting trout from fast and rough water. You can place your dry fly precisely to those lies. You can see your fly, follow it in its drift, and tell when it's been taken by a trout. You can control the float of the fly to achieve a drag-free drift.

When you wade in close, at times standing so your rod tip can be extended directly over the trout you hope to catch, you can notice much more accurately where that trout is likely to hold. When you can look down and spot a submerged boulder on the bottom, you can then drop your dry fly onto whatever tiny hesitation in the current that boulder might cause on the surface. You can sort out conflicting currents at 10 and 20 feet that you would never even notice at 40 and 50 feet and that would defeat you while you wondered why you weren't catching trout.

The main thing you can read when you get up close in rough water is current windows: places where the surface smooths out, due to upwellings, creating a moment of visibility downward for you and upward for trout. These slight slicks, basketball to beachball size, open in the surface and then slide downstream a few feet with the current before closing over again. Trout have a clear sight of anything—a natural or its imitation—sitting on the unruffled surface of such a window. Because of the rougher currents that hem the window in all around, you need to stay back from the opening no more than a rod length or so to stay out of the trout's vision into the outside, aerial world in which you choreograph the dance of your dry fly.

When you're short-lining a dry, you can set the fly accurately onto even a small window, then coax it along, lifting your rod tip high to keep as much line and leader off the water as possible, until the window closes. You will have no trouble seeing the fly, perched there in that calmness surrounded by storm. Trout will see it as well. They'll often rush up to take it.

After reading the water, watching carefully for both lies and opening windows, casting becomes the key to short-line dry-fly fishing. If you're not able to get any accuracy out of your outfit with only a little line out, you won't catch many trout. If your rod is one of the modern distance tools that won't load with just its own length of line beyond the tip guide, try overlining it one line weight. That will usually calm it down and smooth it out. If not, you'll have to try another that will deliver a short cast.

The rod for this kind of fishing should be between 8 and 9 feet long. It's no accident that this is the same rod I've described as being best for fishing along the banks and for presentation fishing as well. If you choose the right trout rod in the first place and line it properly, it will work almost everywhere, and you'll rarely need a caddy to carry any extra rods.

The best leader for short-lining a dry is around 10 feet long, not much longer than the length of the rod. The tippet, critical to a drag-free float, should be at least 2 feet of that. If it gets any shorter, cut it off and start over with 3 feet of whatever size tippet is in balance with the size fly you're using.

Once you're equipped with gear that will handle a short cast, you need to practice the basic casting stroke at rod length to 30 feet until you can place a fly to pinpoint spots on almost every cast. Get the basic forward and backcasts down, short, because you'll use them a lot, and all other short-line casts are built upon them.

The first variation, and the one I use most often, is a kind of quick flick of a power stroke at the very beginning of the forward cast. This abrupt application of power inserts a sudden bend in the tip of the rod rather than loading it smoothly all its length. This slight power, instantly applied and as instantly removed, results in a tight loop. The fly is driven out crisply, turned over briskly, set down gently. This cast works only at short range, because you'd need more power than you can get out of a quick flick to cast farther.

The difficulty is getting the fly to land right where you want it, because the parts of the cast all happen so fast it's impossible to actually sort them out when you're the one doing it. It's similar to firing a rifle by instinct, without taking time to align the sights. That takes practice. It's done by focusing your vision on the target—on a pinpoint part of the whole target—that you'd like to hit, with rifle or fly.

This quick cast is not easy to master. It is somewhat wristy and therefore somewhat wrong. You'd get scolded if you did it during a casting lesson. But once you master it, it will serve you well on fast water, where you're most likely to want to cast short.

Set a dinner plate on your lawn. Get down on one knee not far from it. Begin by holding your rod hand up near your shoulder, with the rod vertical, and tip your head a bit over toward your rod hand to get your eye nearly in line with your cast. Focus on the plate, and make the cast with wristy flicks, forward cast and back, that drive the rod tip in a short arc without changing the position of the butt. When you can tip the rod over and make this cast at a 45- to 60-degree sidearm angle and still hit that dinner plate or come within inches of it, you're about to surprise some fast-water trout.

The second cast to superimpose upon the basic cast, for short-line dry-fly fishing, is one with a wide, looping motion of your entire arm. This is opposite to the abrupt stroke you just finished practicing. The open stroke directs the fly lazily, rather than briskly, to where you want it. The rod tip moves so far that it almost fails to form a loop in the line.

On a short cast, this slow motion lays your line out on the water with lots of the slack that you often need to get a free drift on currents that seethe. If somebody watches you make this cast, they'll laugh right up until the moment they see you set the hook into a trout by doing it.

This lazy cast, like the brisk one before it, has a lot wrong with it, but you need to know it. Practice it standing up, with the rod held high, because that's the way you'll use it on the water most often. Start with a normal backcast, which with a short line does not need to be a strong one. Let your rod drop behind you, as the backcast straightens out, too far for a normal cast. Then loop the rod over, in a long, slow power stroke that goes against everything you've ever been taught about casting.

The rod tip should drive through a full rainbow arc, softly powered all the way—in other words, accelerating from start to finish but never moving very fast. This soft stroke will form a wide, open loop that lobs the fly toward the plate on the lawn or onto a pocket lie on water.

When you're fishing, if there's a breeze blowing, you'll almost always have to adjust this cast for windage, because the line and fly move so slowly. If the wind is at all strong, you'll have to cast with it at your back or give up on this cast entirely. It simply won't get the fly where you want it if the wind is more than moderate.

Once you get your fly onto the water and where you want it, the last element to add is control over its drift. The most important thing you can do to gain that control—a near constant in short-line dry-fly fishing—is to tend your drift with an elevated rod. As soon as the fly lands on the water, lift your rod high and keep as much line and leader off the water as you can. At times—in fact at many, many times—lofting your rod is all you need to do to get a good drift. At other times, you need to apply other techniques.

Control of the line on the water, in short-lining, does not consist of the usual mends and feeding of slack that work with longer casts, usually on smoother water. You need to add a couple techniques that work short but rarely work long.

First, learn a little flick mend that is an extension of the flick cast that might have gotten your fly out there. The instant your initial cast is complete, simply lift the line slightly and send a little ripple down it with a quick up-and-over motion of your wrist. Don't think of this as an upstream or downstream mend. Think, instead, of sending a kink or pigtail down the line as you'd send a hoop down a rope, but tilted to one side or the other to reposition the line in relation to the drift of the fly.

Your line might cross a seam, almost always with the fly on the slow side, the line on the fast side. This would happen, for example, as you fished your way up a pocket behind a boulder in fast water. You would want the fly to drift on the slow water directly in line downstream from the boulder, because that's where you'd expect trout to hold. But it's best to approach such a lie from the side, because the rougher currents there conceal you, while you'd be too exposed to short-line the fish if you waded up the same soft currents in which they held. They'd see you, and that would end that.

When you approach such a lie from the side, your fly lands on slow water, but your line lands on the faster water outside of the lie. The line will move downstream faster than the fly, removing slack from the leader, then dragging the fly. Use the flick mend to bump the line over the seam, into the same current where the fly rides, without tugging at the fly. Many times, you'll not be able to place the line on the same narrow current as the fly, but an upstream flick mend will take tension off the line and give you an extra foot or two of free drift. In a fast-water pocket, that's usually all you need to catch a trout.

This is no normal mend, and in truth, it's more difficult to do. You can't practice it on a lawn, because you need surface tension on the line to execute any mend. Sorry, you'll have to go fishing, work this out on water. I hope no trout interfere with your studies.

The second line-tending technique for short-line dry-fly fishing is a soft, upstream roll cast, moving just enough line to reposition it without moving the leader or fly. You just make the standard roll cast, then weaken it. That's all. You'll use this attenuated roll cast most often when you're fishing upstream, very short, and the line lies on a faster current than the leader and fly. The line begins to race. Just before it straightens the leader and drags the fly, toss an upstream roll to reposition the line and delay drag. This will give you a short but drag-free float.

That's all you're ever after in short-line dry-fly fishing for trout: a short, drag-free float. Learn to position yourself close and correctly, cast short but accurately, and control your drift once your line and fly land on the water. Add these elements together on the kind of water where you're able to stalk up close to trout, and you'll add lots of extra trout to your catch.

8

Slack Line and the Dry Fly

A crisp, accurate cast will drop your dry fly precisely into the feeding lane of a rising trout, onto a promising pinpoint lie, or within the constricted limits of a narrow current seam. This accuracy is the first goal in dry-fly casting. It comes at a slight price.

The cost of crispness and accuracy is a cast that lands on the water with the line and leader straight. When you fish upstream, over a single set of currents that flow downstream toward your rod at an even speed, a straight line and leader will not cause a problem. The drift will introduce its own slack, and you'll get a drag-free drift, which is ultimately what you're after. On any other kind of cast, whether downstream, across stream over currents of different speeds, or even upstream across conflicting currents, you'll be served better by a softer cast that allows the line and leader to land with some slack.

You'll become a far better dry-fly fisherman when you learn to overlay an element of slack on top of your precise, tight-looped dry-fly deliveries. Several methods have been developed to help you install slack in a cast. Each is most useful in a different set of conditions. You'll be served best if you learn them all, and learn beyond that to create your own casts based upon those I'll outline here.

The first, oldest, and in many situations most effective way to lay some slack in a cast is to aim your delivery stroke waist-high and to power it sufficiently that the line loop unfurls completely in the air above the water. This should, indeed, become your standard delivery with a dry fly, executed instinctively unless a situation calls for some other way to make your fly arrive on the water.

When you aim your delivery stroke a bit high, the business end of the cast straightens in the air, then recoils slightly as it drops to the water. The line and leader fall to the water with some natural slack introduced. As a side benefit, far from slight, your fly settles to the water gently. This gentle arrival is often given as the main reason to aim your delivery a bit high. In my opinion, the introduction of slack is more important to your fishing. Taken together, the slack and softness of this type of delivery make it likely to be the one you'll use most often, and with the most success, on upstream presentations with dry flies.

The next most used and perhaps useful method for introducing slack into a dry-fly cast is Mel Krieger's wiggle cast, which I covered at length in chapter 4. It is executed by measuring a few extra feet of line in the air on the forward cast, aiming at the point where you want the fly to land, then waving the rod tip back and forth briskly as the delivery stroke lays out. The line and leader land in a series of S-curves. Without the wobble and consequent wiggle, you'd have a perfect straight-line cast that went a bit beyond your target. You'd quickly get drag.

The wiggle cast is most often used to present a dry fly downstream to a single trout set up in a feeding rhythm in smooth currents. Many other types of casts, however—downstream, cross-stream, and even upstream—can benefit from the addition of slack installed by wiggle in the delivery stroke. That's where you get creative, adding the wiggle whenever you sense you need it. You'll develop that sense after a few refusals. They're usually due to microdrag that you cannot see but the trout can, a problem that is usually solved by casting with some slack.

Another slack-line cast for dry-fly fishing is what I call the "drop and draw," which is based on Art Lee's "stop and drop," outlined in *Fishing Dry Flies for Trout on Rivers and Streams.* Both the stop and drop and the drop and draw are used when fishing dry flies at angles down and across the currents.

In the stop and drop, Lee advises strongly powering the forward cast and lowering the rod tip as the delivery stroke slides out. When the line is almost all out, in the air, the rod tip is raised abruptly. This stops the line suddenly in the air and causes it to drop to the water with slack. You then lower the rod tip and extend your arm to follow the float of the fly, extending its free drift.

In the drop and draw, the power stroke is made more gently. At the same time that the line loop lays out and the line slides through the guides, you drop the rod tip until it points straight down the line and draw the rod back until the reel is at your hip or even behind it. The rod is held low and back at the end of the cast, much as John Wayne might point his pistol to shoot from the hip. Taking the power off the stroke while letting the line slide introduces slack. As this slack on the water plays out and the fly floats downstream, you can again reach forward with your rod to extend the drag-free drift.

The drop and draw is not quite as accurate as the wiggle cast. It works best in situations where the water is a bit rough, the feeding lanes not precisely defined. I often use it to search riffles and runs with downstream casts, where I want the fly to appear to the trout ahead of the line and leader, not trailing along behind them as it would on upstream casts to the same drift lines. You can normally do well enough fishing the dry fly upstream on riffles, but some waters are so heavily pestered these days that switching to tactics you'd usually use on smooth water pays off in the rough.

On the Bighorn River not long ago, I waded into the downstream end of a slightly chopped riffle with some caddis on the water, some nice noses poking out to intercept them now and then. It seemed like a classic situation for a size 16 Deer Hair Caddis fished with casts up and across stream. I tried that and was surprised to fail. I was about to nip off the fly and try another, but I saw no reason that the fly was wrong, and I knew that riffle got fished several times a day by guides and anglers passing by in boats.

Rather than change flies, I waded out, walked up to the head of the riffle, and began fishing it downstream, covering all of the water with the drop and draw. I did not do astoundingly well, but about a dozen of those noses got tweaked in the next pleasant hour.

Another useful method for introducing slack is the "pile cast," executed by taking power off the normal delivery stroke so early that the last few feet of line and the leader tower almost straight in the air over the aiming point. The line and leader accordion down to the water in a slightly extended pile. With practice, you will learn to make the fly land by itself just on the far side of the stacked line and leader.

The pile cast is effective on trout feeding in eddies alongside fast currents, where you have to lay your line over the fast current but get a drift, or more often simply a moment of sit, on the slow water. The pile cast also works for trout sipping on the slow inside edge of a current seam that you cannot reach without placing your line across the faster outside current. In both of these cases, the fly lands on slow water and the line on fast water. Those vastly conflicting currents draw the line tight and cause almost instant drag with any normal cast, or even with a wiggle cast. The pile cast will usually give you a brief drag-free float before the line tugs the slack out of the leader and races the fly out of there. Often that's enough to catch trout you otherwise would not.

A final (though I should not use that word, for there are other techniques I don't use myself and will not cover) method to add to your repertoire of slack-line casts is the "bounce cast," made simply by laying out the normal brisk dry-fly cast, then giving the delivery stroke a bit of a backward jolt when the line is almost straight but still above the water. This recoil causes the line and leader to land with slack.

The jolt can be made by bouncing the line with the rod tip, in which case the bounce cast looks a lot like Art Lee's stop and drop. The bounce can also be made by giving the line a twitch with your line hand while the rod is aimed down the line and the forecast has just unfurled, before it drops to the water. This is a more subtle movement and somewhat more difficult to learn to time. It gives you a bit more control over where the fly will land, as opposed to a bounce installed by the rod tip. But the bounce cast is never very accurate and is best used when covering water, not pinpointing rises.

Precision does not come without practice with any of these slack-line casts. That is why I said at the first that slack is a factor you want to learn to overlay on accuracy in your casting. Strive for mastery of the basic casting stroke, with its tight loop and consequent straight line and leader. Once you can execute it consistently and with grace at trout-fishing ranges—shorter and therefore easier than you've been led to believe—learn to add slack in the different ways mentioned while maintaining accuracy and control.

None of these slack-line casts will serve you very well the first time you apply them against selective, snotty trout, which are the ones the casts are designed to help you fool. All require practice, whether on a lawn, over a casting pond, or in a situation where trout are rising and you must install some slack or fail to catch them.

We tend to think that slack-line casts are useful only for fishing downstream to rising trout or casting across conflicting currents. But the usefulness of slack-line casts is not limited to those kinds of situations. It often helps to add slack even on an upstream cast over currents that appear to be without conflict but are not. Invisible microcurrents often seethe in all sorts of directions. If these tug your tippet tight, you'll get drag without ever noticing it.

I've learned over many years, too many of them arrogantly thinking that the native cutts in my favorite plunge-pool hill streams were stupid, that some slack added to my upstream casts will give me better floats even down dashing current tongues. It's not the kind of water where you'd think a little drag would bother trout. But when I began adding slack, I realized that a lot of those slashing missed rises that I had always supposed to be mistimings on the part of the trout had actually been rejections on account of drag. And I began hooking those trout. Perversely, I concluded that the trout had suddenly become smarter, when in fact they'd stayed the same.

9

Subsurface Situations and Solutions

Trout often feed just beneath the surface, but by the nature of what's going on, it appears that they're taking on the top, not under it. My instinct in such a situation, and I suspect yours as well, is to give it a glance and assume the trout are taking whatever insect is in the air or on the water. I tie on a dry fly, wade in, begin casting, and often catch nothing but frustration.

Solving the problem, when trout appear to feed on top but do not, is most often a matter of observing more closely to see what is truly happening, then rerigging a bit to present a fly where trout are actually doing their feeding: subsurface. Let's look at three common cases.

The first is a searching situation, with no consistent hatch happening but a small variety of insects in the air and occasionally on the water. It's usually on a small stream but can also occur on any size freestone stream or river or on the faster parts of any tailwater or even spring creek. Trout rise sporadically, not with any rhythm, and you move along slowly as you should, fishing a searching dry fly such as a size 12 to 16 Adams, Royal Wulff, Elk

Hair Caddis, or slightly larger Stimulator. You read the water and cast carefully to all the likely lies of trout. Once in a while, you move into position to cover a trout that just revealed its precise lie by setting some rise rings spreading on the surface.

What you get for all your wading and casting is nothing but constant splashy rises. At first you think you're setting the hook too slowly to the takes. You react more quickly, but that just blows your fly out of there and puts the fish down. That makes you think you're setting the hook too fast. You recite some mantra of your own devising before you raise the rod to draw the hook home—the British use "God save the queen!"—but the fly still skates away.

This sort of situation happens most often when the sun is bright. I don't understand it entirely, but I do know that in searching situations, with no hatch going on and the sun bright, trout often become bashful about the surface. I've crept near and watched these trout at work. What they're doing is rejecting the dry fly at the last instant, sending a rise or even a splash boiling up around it. You set the hook, but the trout didn't take, so naturally you miss no matter how swiftly or slowly you strike. Calm down. Go back to setting the hook your old way. That is not the problem, and this is not your fault.

The prescribed solution to refusal rises is to tie on a smaller and/or drabber dry fly. That can work, and you should try it. More often, however, I've found that the solution lies in presenting a fly subsurface rather than on top. My preferred method to accomplish this on a small stream, or in fast water on any size or shape stream, is to nip off the searching dry, tie on a size 12 or 14 Partridge and Yellow soft-hackled wet, and continue fishing it just as if it were the dry I'd just been using: casting upstream, letting the fly drift downstream just inches deep.

Trout seem to lose their bashfulness as soon as the fly is sunk. They rush it, take it, trot off with it. If the pool or piece of water you're fishing holds more than one trout, they'll all rush it. If you can creep close enough and refrain from setting the hook, you can entertain yourself watching their quarrels over your fly. Suddenly you're catching fish, which, if you're a fisherman, is one of the ways to say you're having fun.

In the second subsurface situation, trout hold high in the water column and work visibly in their feeding lanes, taking something without much movement from side to side. As often as not, they tip up toward the top to feed, and that sends a swirl to the surface. It looks precisely like a dry-fly take, one to be solved with a tiny dry or emerger dressing. There is almost always a hatch, usually of mayflies or midges, going on when trout feed in this way, and the trout feed as if they're taking the floating adults.

They might be. You should always try to solve the situation with a dry fly or surface film emerger first. But one or the other will not always work. When they do not, it's still correct that the trout are feeding on the hatch. The only adjustment you need to make is in your assumption about what stage of the hatch they're taking. Trout often concentrate on mayfly nymphs or midge pupae as they lift toward the surface for emergence into the winged adult stage. The take then is actually subsurface, though it sends a riseform to the top.

Two bits of observation will tell you when this sort of feeding is taking place. The first is a lack of insects disappearing off the surface. Get close or use binoculars, and follow the careers of a few floating naturals. If you see swirls but no victims disappearing, it's likely trout are feeding subsurface, not on top. The second hint is the absence of bubbles in the rise rings left after a take. Again, you must look closely. If a trout takes something off the surface or in the film, it takes in air and releases it on the way down. If it does not break the surface plane, then the bubbles are missing and the take is subsurface.

Having determined that these visible and apparently rising trout are actually feeding beneath the surface, it is easy enough to associate the adult insect with its previous stage. If mayflies are hatching, tie on a mayfly nymph. Or try a tangled flymph or soft-hackled wet to represent a dun that has left its nymphal shuck in the few inches of water just beneath the surface and must struggle the rest of the way to the top with legs and wings and tails all awash in the water. If midges are hatching, tie on a pupa pattern.

Present these subsurface patterns upstream, just as if you were still fishing a dry fly. Treat your leader with fly floatant all the way to the tippet knot to suspend your nymph or wet fly just a few inches deep. If you have trouble detecting takes, use a dry fly or a small tuft of yarn 4 to 6 feet up the leader for an indicator. Be sure to place the fly right into those feeding lanes. These trout will not move far to either side to take anything, even a natural.

The third and final situation I'll cover is somewhat simple. You see adult caddisflies in the air, usually in the afternoon or evening, usually on water that is a bit rough: a riffle or fast run on any kind of stream or river. You see sporadic splashy rises, what Gary LaFontaine in *Caddisflies* calls pyramid rises, for the little peaks of water they send into the air. You try a dry fly but trout ignore it, or they take it so seldom that you think you should be doing better. That's likely true.

The problem is that most trout stream feeding to caddis is either to pupae on their trip to the top for emergence or to adults on their swim to the bottom to lay their eggs. You see adults in the air, and it seems the rising trout are taking them off the surface. At times they are, and a dry fly will work. That's why you should always try a dry fly first when you get into one of these situations. But trout often concentrate their feeding on pupae or diving adults, in which case your best effort to match the adult with a floating fly will fall flat. You need to imitate either pupae or diving adults.

Caddis pupae are difficult to observe. They swim right up and pop through the surface, then the adult emerges quickly and flies away. You never see them, but trout do. Sometimes trout intercept pupae so near the top that the takes send little jets of water into the air—pyramid rises. Whenever you see such vigorous feeding and observe caddis adults in the air, switch to a pupa pattern and fish it beneath the surface.

Soft-hackled wets work well when this is going on. But I've always had my best luck with olive-, tan-, brown-, or orange-bodied Sparkle Pupa dressings. Since it's so hard to collect the transitional natural, and I have personal reservations about pumping trout stomachs, my way to arrive at the right one is to start with the olive, try the tan if it fails, and so on until I find the one that works.

I always tie these flies slightly weighted, to get them a few inches deep, and fish them on a floating line and dry-fly leader. I've had some luck fishing them upstream to rises, but since rises are usually so sporadic when adult caddis are in the air, I've had more consistent success fishing them on the traditional downstream wet-fly swing. Natural caddis pupae are normally at the will of the currents. The more slowly the imitation can be fished, the faster the fishing usually turns out to be. So I mend the line almost constantly to slow the swim of the fly on its swing down and around, then I wait while the line straightens out in the current directly downstream from me, in case a trout has followed and decides to take only when what it mistakes to be a caddis pupa appears to be about to escape.

Females of the two most important groups of trout stream caddis, gray sedges *(Rhyacophila)* and spotted sedges *(Hydropsyche)*, lay their eggs by diving into the water, swimming down to the bottom, and attaching their eggs to bottom stones. A few of these adults will fail in their attempts to bat themselves through the surface and will wind up afloat on top. Trout will take them there whenever they get a chance. That's why you'll catch a few trout on dry flies when this is happening. But most trout concentrate on diving adults and feed subsurface.

When you see caddis adults in the air, it's simple to collect a specimen in your hand or hat, then switch from the dry fly to a soft-hackled wet, winged wet, or flymph about the same size and color as the adult you've captured. You need make no changes in your rigging. Nip off the dry. Tie on the wet. You're ready to swim your subsurface imitation of the adult.

Fish it on a slow swing across and downstream, just as you would a Sparkle Pupa. This kind of simple but pleasant and productive wet-fly fishing is often denigrated as mere "chuck and chance it." But when caddis adults are on the wing and trout are on the prowl, it's no accident that trout ignore a dry fly but eagerly accept a wet fly fished shallow and on the swing.

When trout are feeding subsurface, in what appears to be a dry-fly situation, you'll catch more if you pay attention and adjust what you're doing to the level at which they're feeding. Whether they're splashing sporadically at a variety of insects, focused and sipping during a hatch of mayflies or midges, or taking subsurface but with spurting rises while caddis adults cavort in the air above the stream, you'll do better with nymphs or wets than you will with drys.

10

Nymphs on the Swing

I met Ernest "Tex" Baxter, a retired Air Force sergeant, along an abandoned stretch of the lower Big Hole River. It was September, in the early 1970s. I had set up camp in a cottonwood grove at the edge of the river and stayed in that shaded bit of heaven for several weeks.

Nobody else seemed to be fishing that entire reach of river, but one morning I hiked upstream from camp and beheld Tex standing in a broad, sunstruck riffle playing a trout. I stopped on the bleached gravel bar behind him to watch. We got to talking after he released the fish, a fat rainbow a full 16 inches long. Tex said he'd hooked it on a nymph, an accomplishment that was a surprise to me then.

Tex had his tent trailer tucked into a cottonwood grove on the opposite side of the river from my camp. We wound up meeting mornings on the river and fishing in a sort of loose tandem for two days, and we remained friends for many years. I've retained ever since that time together, and apply often to this day, a simple but far from small thing that Tex taught me about nymphing for trout. But he didn't tell it to me.

The second morning, we met and ambled slowly upstream along one of the wide gravel bars that sweep away from the Big Hole in fall, when the water is low, drawn down by irrigation. We arrived at a great expanse of broken riffle, too rough and rushing to fish well with a dry fly, even a heavily hackled one. It was the kind of water I'd have glanced at and walked past—and was about to, as Tex could tell. It looked too fast to hold trout in the limited fishing experience I'd had at that time.

Tex set his brakes at the head of this riffle and said, "I'm going to nymph here for a while. You go on if you want."

That puzzled me. A few early and breathless articles on nymphing had appeared in the general outdoor magazines of the time, back before there were any fly-fishing magazines. All the articles I read pontificated that you fished nymphs on upstream casts, just like dry flies, and watched your floating line tip or leader for any twitch of a take on the subsequent downstream drift. It made excellent theory then and still does, if the water is shaped just right for it: relatively smooth and with trout working to naturals near the surface. But it didn't work for me in the rougher water I fished most often, where I tried the method and failed. I found it frustrating and futile and abruptly gave up on nymphs.

When Tex said he was about to nymph that riffle, his announcement was set against my failure to have any luck on nymphs except bad. I was astonished by both his confidence and his casualness about it. The way he said he was going to nymph the riffle implied that he was also going to catch some trout when he did it. I did not go on. I sat on some hard rocks at the head of that riffle to watch him fish it, prepared for epiphany.

It didn't arrive at that instant.

All Tex did was wade a few feet out in the shallow water at the head of the riffle, cast a little downstream from straight across the current, and follow with his rod while his fly washed down and around below him. I was disappointed. He'd failed to wade in at the tail end of the riffle and fish it with upstream casts, as those articles said he should.

My disappointment was little lessened by his elevation and exercise of trout after fat trout as Tex worked slowly down that riffle, fishing in discord with all that I'd read. Something accidental was happening here, was my take on it all, and I still recall a vague sense that I'd better get out of there before I got corrupted by it. I felt mildly jilted rather than enlightened.

I left Tex and wandered upstream until I found water suited to my Catskill and Wulff dry flies, where I did almost as well as Tex was doing with his nymphs down in that unfishable riffle. I was not struck by epiphany until a long time later—years, I'll confess—when I finally realized that more can be learned by watching somebody who knows what he's doing, wet in water and catching trout, than can ever be absorbed through an article in a magazine or a chapter in a book.

Catching trout on nymphs, Tex had taught me by doing it, can be kept quite simple.

Why does simply fishing nymphs on the swing, like old-fashioned wet flies, work so well? First, because a myriad of natural nymphs and larvae cut themselves loose from their streambed or weed-bed moorings almost daily in what entomologists call behavioral drift. Trout see a lot of naturals, especially at morning and evening, drifting placidly downstream toward whatever fate the currents might deliver them, whether to new and greener aquatic pastures or into the jaws of hungry trout. Second, a nymph on the swing works because so many insect adults, both aquatic and terrestrial, fall or dive or die on the water, early, late, or during the heart of the day, and are drowned. These are also escorted along at the speed of the current. Ragged fur nymphs look sufficiently like drowned adults, in rough water, to fool fish.

The very variety of ways for insects to arrive in their feeding lies adds up to trout seeing and eating drifting insects of scattered sizes and shapes and kinds all during the average day. When you swing a nymph in front of a trout and the trout rushes to accept it, it's no accident happening. It's the re-creation with an artificial fly of an event that occurs constantly with naturals.

Selecting nymph patterns that work well on the swing is easy. Trout are not often selective when feeding on the drift, especially in brisk and broken water. If you've already got favorites, use them and they'll work best for you. If you do not, I recommend a few patterns that cover nature's repeated color themes: the Gold-Ribbed Hare's Ear (brown), Dave Whitlock's Fox Squirrel (tan), the old standard Gray Nymph, and the Herl Nymph (olive). Weight them moderately. Tie them in sizes 12 to 16, and use them smaller than you think you should for the water in which you're fishing. You're now armed and dangerous.

Rigging to fish nymphs on the swing is too straightforward to be anything but brief about. Use the same floating line and dry-fly leader you've already got spooled on your reel. If you desire to fish deep, you can use a wet-tip line and shorten the leader. However, if the water is so deep or swift that you need a wet-tip to get down, consider rigging with a strike indicator and split shot instead, and fish upstream, not down on the swing.

You've chosen a nymph now and are rigged to fish it on the swing. Before stepping in to begin casting, let's step back and notice how a perfect piece of water for the method is shaped. You don't want to fish this way in water where another method might work better.

A shallow, broken riffle is ideal for a nymph on the swing. The reasons, like the method, are simple. Riffles are the richest sections of any stream—with the exception of weed beds in streams that have them—in terms of aquatic insects. Trout see a wide variety of little lives there and are accustomed to feeding without becoming selective. A riffle is by definition water moving briskly. Trout don't get much time to make decisions. They'll move swiftly to almost any reasonable fly and, I'm sorry to say, at times to some unreasonable ones, and at times they'll even take with thumps. Most often, though, they'll accept the fly as the current delivers it, and the take amounts to something soft, even in fast water.

The ideal water would be shallow: 1 to 3 feet deep, never more than 4. A nymph on the swing, fished with a floating line, does not sink more than inches. If the water drops off much more than 4 feet, trout will fail to notice the nymph passing overhead or will see it but refuse to move so far for such a small particle of nutrition. Once again, if you need to get deep, forget this method and fish with another, usually shot and indicator.

Now wade in and make your cast. But don't wade in right at the head of the riffle, stepping into what I call the riffle corner, and therefore onto the heads of trout. That's a prime lie, where the largest trout often hang out because they want to nose up to where they get first crack at whatever food gets delivered down from the water upstream. Take your initial position, as Tex taught me by example, a short cast upstream from the first water in the riffle where you suspect a trout might lie.

Make that first cast short, into water that flows directly into the water you want to fish first. Let the current escort the fly downstream and around, cutting right across the seam from fast water out in the riffle itself to the slower water on the inside edge of the riffle. The most likely single instant for a strike is that moment when the fly swims across the seam between fast water and slow, though a trout might take at any time.

Remember that sequence in Ray Bergman's *Trout*, in which he hid in the brush next to a classic pool and watched while a parade of anglers came along and fished it wrong? If you were to plant yourself next to a riffle on the Big Hole, Madison, Beaverkill, Ausable, or Au Sable, you would watch nine anglers out of ten wade precisely into the riffle corner, scattering trout, and casting out beyond it, not necessarily catching naught but not catching all they could. Scout that seam at the head of every riffle you intend to fish, no matter how you intend to fish it. If you're about to fish it with a nymph on the swing, take up a position upstream from the highest lie to make your nymph swing across the seam and into it.

The fly must swim slowly, like a natural nymph might. That requires an addition to the simple swing. When your line bellies downstream, flip it into an upstream mend to slow the fly. Repeat mending as needed, which in perfect water for fishing a nymph on the swing means almost constantly. Make your cast a few feet either upstream or downstream from straight across. Give your fly a few feet of drift to sink, make a mend, and follow it with more mends until the fly crosses that seam between fast water and slow.

Let the fly swim idly into the slow water for at least a foot or two. Take a step or two. Pick up gently; never rip the line off the water. Cast again at the same angle across the current. Let the fly sink, mend, and mend again. When a trout strikes, don't jerk. The trout will set the hook itself. Yank and you'll break it off, but I'll never be the one to scold you for that. If I told you it took me twenty years, after that first lesson from Tex, to learn not to react with excitement when a trout accepts my nymph on the swing, I'd be lying.

I haven't learned it yet.

11

Slicks in Riffled Water

Nearly every broad riffle and many small ones have slight slick areas sprinkled across their surfaces. At times these are windows that open and slide down the riffle at the speed of the current before slowly closing again. Such windows are excellent places on which to set a dry fly, because trout can peer up and see it clearly, and will often arrow up and strike it swiftly. But moving windows tell you little about the bottom down below.

Stationary slicks tell a far different story. From the top, you see a smooth area of current surrounded by the typical choppy waves of the riffle. The slick is usually longer than it is broad, anywhere from a foot to 5 feet wide across the current, 3 to 20 or even 30 feet long down the length of it. The normal thinking is that if you peered at the bottom, you'd see a submerged boulder interrupting the current and causing the slick. Many times that is true. Other times it's not. If it's a boulder, you'll probably see at least a slight boil at the head of the slick. You should fish carefully both upstream and down from that boil, because trout hold upstream and down from a boulder on the bottom.

A slick on the surface of a riffle is caused just as often by a bottom that drops away from the rest of the bottom around it. The surrounding shallow and rocky bottom is reflected by the bumpy waves up top. Where the bottom drops away into a trench, it is reflected by a window of smoothness on the surface, but one that is stationary rather than moving downstream with the current.

It's important that you learn to recognize and then to scout out and fish these slicks because of what they tell you about the bottom. Wherever you find a trench in fast water, whether it's 3 feet or 30 feet long, whether it's just a foot deeper than the water around it or the bottom drops into a trough 5 feet deeper than the water surrounding it, you're likely to find one or more trout hanging out. The current is softened. Nature delivers lots of food over the lip of the trench. Living is easy there if you're a trout in a riffle.

Territory increases as a factor in trout behavior as water speed accelerates. Trout in lakes and ponds travel in schools. Trout in slow to still pools gather in groups. Trout in runs hold in twos and threes above and below boulders and other obstructions. Trout in riffles spread out as individuals in typical small holding lies. That's all an oversimplification, but give trout a trench that slows the current in a riffle, and they often line up, the number depending on the size of the holding lie.

What you already know about territoriality tells you that trout in a trench line up roughly in order of size. It also tells you that the biggest trout in any riffle is likely to be the one holding first below the lip of the trench you've just discovered by noticing a slight slick on the surface of the riffle in which you're wading. What do you do to tempt that trout out of there? The obvious answer is to drop a streamer or nymph over the lip and into the trench.

The late Polly Rosborough, author of *Tying and Fishing the Fuzzy Nymphs,* was expert at fishing streamers over trenches in his home Williamson River, in southern Oregon. That broad river's riffles are mostly shallow volcanic baserock, lined with trenches. Big rainbow trout, remnants of a summer steelhead stock landlocked by a natural landslide that formed Klamath Lake, move up into the river on foraging and spawning runs.

Polly fished his big streamers unweighted, but on a wet-tip line and stout 5- to 6-foot leader. He got into position above a trench and at an angle off to the side. He cast far upstream from the slick that marked the trench, mended his line while the fly got right down against the bottom, then gave his rod tip a slow and rhythmic 1-foot circular motion that caused the fly to swim and rest, swim and rest.

Polly's goal was to swing the fly over the lip or edge of a trench and have it fall right in. His flies, tied on size 2 to 6 long-shank hooks, were large enough to entice trout up a bit if the fly failed to sink to their level. His method worked well for the large and predatory trout he was after and will work for you if you fish big water for big fish.

Spring spawning runs of rainbows and fall runs of browns, out of reservoirs or natural lakes, leap to mind as perfect places to apply Polly's method. For more typical fish that live year-round in riffles and make their daily living eating insects, you might be better served with a nymphing method that is designed to excavate trenches.

For nymphing most trenches, you probably just need to pinch an extra shot onto the typical split shot and strike indicator rig you're already using to fish the riffle surrounding the trench. If that's not what you're using, let me give you the setup: floating line, leader 8 to 10 feet long, strike indicator two to three times the water depth up the leader, your favorite nymph tied to the tippet 10 inches to a foot from the number of split shot it takes to get the fly to tap along the bottom.

You might also try a two-nymph rig, giving the trout a choice. It's unlikely a trout in a trench in a riffle is going to be selective, but it might be happier to get a large nymph than a small one, a bright nymph than a drab one, a standard nymph rather than a beadhead. Rig with a salmonfly nymph and small nymph as trailer, a bright scud and drab Pheasant Tail, or a Hare's Ear and the beadhead of your choice, and trout can sort out the fly they like.

Reading the lie right and taking the proper position to fish it are likely more important than choosing the fly or flies with which you'll tempt the trout. Wade as close as you dare without risking spooking the trout holding in the lie. Your position should be off to the side, not at the downstream end of the slick, but just downstream from its head. You want your first casts to deliver the nymph over the lip of the trench. Avoid the normal procedure of fishing the lie with successive casts working up from the lower end. If you do that, you'll catch the smaller trout at the least end of the trench and thereby alarm those at the plentiful upper end. Your first cast should be aimed for splash-in a few feet upstream from the trench, so you don't frighten the one trout you'd most like to catch.

If I were to try to put it precisely, you should be about 20 feet downstream and the same distance off to the side from the lip of a typical trench. A 30-foot cast will then place the fly 10 feet upstream from the lip and give it time to sink to the bottom before it gets there. Again, that's all theory. As we used to say in the infantry, it depends on the situation. If the water is faster, you'll need to cast farther upstream from the lip of the trench. If the water is slower, you might use less weight to maintain the same distance upstream, or shorten the landing distance to about 5 feet upstream from the trench.

You make similar adjustments for depth. If the water is deep, use more weight or cast farther upstream. If it's shallow, use less weight or cast closer to the lip of the trench. Your goal is to get the nymph or nymphs to the bottom just upstream from the lip of the trench. When the fly reaches the lip, it should drop right in. Of course, you're trying to accomplish this though you cannot see exactly what is happening down there. Use your imagination, which is part of what separates you from trout and most of what joins you to them.

As soon as you've made your cast, steal a page from John Judy's book *Slack Line Strategies,* and throw a roll-cast mend that places your line upstream from the strike indicator. This gives the indicator, and therefore also the fly, a free drift. The fly arrives more naturally and is also more likely to drop into the trench rather than to be suspended along above it.

After the cast and roll-cast mend, you have nothing to do but tend the drift as the fly approaches the trench. Lift your rod to keep as much line as possible off the water. Make further mends if the line begins to belly. Lower your rod slowly after the indi-cator passes your position. Fish out as much of the length of the trench as you can on each cast and drift. Feed line into the drift as long as the fly is in productive water and fishing correctly below you. When the drift is played out, stop the rod, let the current lift the shot and fly, then cast again.

Adjust your aiming point upstream or down, depending on whether the fly has hit bottom too soon, too late, or never at all.

Your goal is to have it touch down just before it tumbles over the lip. It's most likely that you'll have to cast higher into the current than you'd suspect. It's certain that the only way you'll know you hit bottom is a hesitation in the float of your indicator. You've got no choice then but to set the hook, because it might be a trout. If it is, which it will be often, I hope that doesn't disappoint you.

It takes some experimenting to get the rigging, cast, and drift right for each trench that you encounter. It takes some experience to learn to spot and then to correctly rig and fish trenches as a water type inset in riffles.

The best way to fish these trenches—the easiest way to scope out the right rigging, position, and cast—is to take each as you encounter it in the process of fishing the riffle around it. Already rigged to fish the bottom in water that is just a bit shallower, you spot a slick, recognize that it denotes a trench, move into position to drop a nymph over the lip of it, and now all you've got to do is add that extra shot that you know will drop the fly into the trench and then into the welcoming jaws of a waiting trout.

On big water, or even a medium stream, that trout might be a big one. But even on a small stream, where trout diets are somewhat restricted and maximum sizes attained are not often awesome, the lead trout in a trench might be an exception to the average size of the trout all around it, just as the place that holds it is a bit deeper than the water that surrounds it.

Small streams have as many trenches as bigger water, maybe more. They're denoted by the same indicator: a slick on the surface. But the trenches are usually more compact and seated in more vigorous settings, so spotting the slicks over them takes a more practiced eye. You've got to learn to look for a soft spot the size of a desktop at biggest, a coffee-table top on the average. Most are elongated, the length up- and downstream a greater dimension than the width across stream, but at times not by much. In lots of fast water, a slick might be round and no bigger than a basketball hoop.

All of these lies will hold trout, some of them lots of trout. They will be distributed the same as in a large river: biggest first and smaller trout lined up behind it, though if you took a snapshot it's likely they would not show in it so clearly aligned. The world of water is always shifting, which is one reason you fish trenches in small, swift streams: They're stationary lies in all that seething water around them.

You can fish small-stream trenches with a dry fly, if trout are willing to strike up to the top, because they don't usually have as far to go as they would in a large river. But the subject here is nymphing, and you might rig a bit differently to nymph trenches in smaller water.

My favorite way to do it is with a single size 12 beadhead nymph or a weighted size 12 to 14 standard nymph. These have enough inherent weight to sink a couple feet if you give them enough time, thus allowing you to dispense with the split shot necessary on larger streams. That reduces tangles in situations where you often must make tight-looped little casts. It also reduces hang-ups on the bottom, which would be common if you used split shot in water that is just a foot or so deep above the lip of a trench that drops to just a couple of feet deep. I use a bright yarn strike indicator 3 to 4 feet up the leader from the nymph, though a hard indicator might work as well for you.

The final difference between fishing big-water trenches and those in small streams is the distance from which you approach them. On big water, you get back 30 feet or so and lob from there. On small water, especially where the trench is surrounded by frothed whitewater, more often you'll want to get right up next to the trench, one or two rod lengths away, off to the side and a bit toward the downstream end. That lets you drop a cast accurately to the water 2 to 5 feet upstream from where you assess the lip of the trench to be.

As your nymph settles to the water and begins to sink, make a small flip mend to set the indicator upstream from it. Then watch the indicator carefully as it follows the nymph down toward the lip of the trench. You'll be startled at how often your indicator takes a swift dip, and you'll be surprised at how consistently the trout that caused its disappearance proves to be larger than the average you're used to catching from such small water.

12

Early-Season
Streamer Tactics

In early-season streamer time, the water, depending on pre-vailing weather, will be high and cold or low and cold. In either case, trout will be on the bottom, moving little. But they'll move if a sizable fly is delivered in a way that tempts them to take it. Your goal becomes focused on just two points: get your fly on or very near the bottom, and fish it slowly enough that trout don't need to chase it. You reach this two-pronged goal in different ways on waters of different sizes.

Small waters, so cramped that you cannot position your-self to cast across their pools, must be approached from either upstream or down. An approach from downstream, wading up, is better because it lets you cast upstream and fish your fly down with the current, in the direction an injured baitfish might move.

Most foothill and mountain creeks have well-defined stair-step pools. Most small-stream trout, and almost always the larg-est of them, hang under current tongues toward the heads of these pools, in spring, where they can be first to intercept food delivered down the current.

Rig to fish pools in small waters with a floating 4- or 5-weight line, a leader the length of the rod, which should usually be 7 to 8 feet long, and a relatively small streamer, size 10 or 12, weighted out of proportion to its size. My favorite is a Lead-Eyed Woolly Bugger in olive or black. Whatever streamer you use must plunge the instant it hits.

Move into your casting position at the foot of a pool. If you're after lots of fish and not concerned about size, fan your casts upstream to cover the tailout, the water along the edges, and the lower part of the main current slot. Extend your final casts to place the fly right where the water enters the pool. If the pool is long, which will be rare, you might have to reposition yourself partway up the pool to accomplish this. Always retrieve back down toward you, taking in line just a bit faster than the current escorts the fly, to keep it off the bottom and looking alive.

If you're after that one largest trout in the pool, calculate your first cast to catch it. Make it straight up the current line, over the deepest water, directly to the head of the pool, where the current comes in. Give the heavy fly a moment to sink; it shouldn't need more, and it might thud to the bottom and simply sit if you allow it to sink too long.

Retrieve downstream just fast enough to keep the fly out of trouble with the bottom. The streamer will nod and bob down the length of the current line, which is not accidentally the deepest slot in almost all pools, and the delivery system as well for almost all of the food that enters a pool. That one big trout—always relative to the size of the stream it is in—will usually be first to see the fly when it arrives this way and will surely be tempted to take the streamer stumbling toward it.

Trout streams of medium size, defined as being about a cast across, should be fished with streamers using a fast-sinking wet-tip or wet-head line in 5- or 6-weight, the rod 8 to 9 feet long. Shorten the leader to 6 or 7 feet. Choose a streamer that is more the swimming type than a bottom bouncer. A weighted size 6, 8, or 10 Mickey Finn, Muddler, or Black Marabou Muddler should work well, though if you've got favorites, they'll always work best for you, and you should use them.

Pools are not always well defined in streams of average size, with gentler gradients than smaller streams higher up in watersheds. You might discover yourself casting streamers over riffles with trenches sprinkled down them, runs studded by boulder lies, and bend pools where the sweeping current pushes the depths up against the outside bank.

Take up your first casting position in any of these types of water straight across the currents from the water where you want your fly to begin to fish. Refrain from wading in until you've made at least a few casts to cover the water near you. The water on your side of the stream has just as much potential to hold trout, if it has any depth, as the greener pastures across the pool.

Cover all of the water with a fan of casts, starting short and working subsequent casts farther out. Place each cast at an angle slightly upstream from your position. Give the line that early upstream part of the drift to tug the fly down. When the line lies straight across the currents, then begins to swing downstream, take up the slack to bring your rod tip into closer contact with the fly. Make sure the fly swings just above each bit of bottom.

Coax the streamer slowly into an arc down and around, all across the riffle, run, or pool. Make upstream mends to keep your line from forming a downstream belly, thus dropping the fly deeper and slowing its swing.

After you've covered all the water you can reach with easy casts from your first casting position, move downstream about the distance of half to two-thirds of a cast, and begin covering all of the water once more, from near to far. By wading down less than the distance of a full cast, your casting fans overlap, and you cover all of the water thoroughly, which is necessary when you fish water where the obvious lies are not all clearly marked. Trout might be anywhere out there, and you want to be sure each has a chance to accept your fly without the need to hunt it down.

Most hits will happen at one of two times: first, when the streamer inserts itself into any holding lie, such as a trench or boulder pocket (not all of these will be visible, but some will be marked by slicks or boils on the surface), and second, when the fly swims out of the main current and crosses the seam into the slow water alongside it, almost straight downstream from you, at the end of the swing. If you drop your rod tip, toss some slack, or make a slight mend at either of these two moments, the streamer will hesitate. This makes it look like something easy to eat that has suddenly stumbled into a trout's area of opportunity.

When you fish a big river with streamers, it's probable that your own opportunities will include a chance at the largest trout. Do all you can to enhance that chance. Avoid idle time with your streamer stranded in the mid-depths by choosing a line that will escort it directly to the bottom. Use a Cortland Quick Descent 175, Teeney 200, Scientific Anglers ST200, or a line with similar abrupt-sinking characteristics on a 9- to 10-foot rod that is strong enough to propel it. Stub the leader to just 4 to 6 feet. Use heavily weighted size 2, 4, and 6 streamers in either swimming or bottom-bouncing styles. Muddlers and other sculpin styles work well in most big waters.

The best streamer water in an average big river is typically a long, almost featureless run of almost even depth, usually 4 to 8 feet. Trout hold on the bottom upstream and down from boulders that break the steady current or in slight trenches in the bottom. Such lies in big water are rarely marked on the surface in a way that is easily readable, so you have no choice but to cover all of the water. Let your fly search out the holding lies for you.

Sometimes you'll find true pools—water that drops off deeper than that upstream and down from it—in big rivers. But large rivers are at the downstream, low-gradient ends of their own systems; they have worked at their bottom contours for eons, and pools are actually rather rare. What we call bend pools are common, but in truth they're runs with the main current, and therefore the greatest depth, pushed to the outside edge. The rules for fishing them remain the same as for runs of even depth or runs a bit deeper under a central or main current.

Take up your initial position at the upper end of the stretch of water you desire to fish. Step on in if it's wadable; the trout you're after will be out where it's deeper when you're in a streamer situation, which is usually defined by an absence of signs, such as rising trout, that some other method will work better. Make your initial casts short, either slightly up- or downstream from straight across. You'll have to search for the casting angle that delivers the fly to the bottom in the depth and current speed you're fishing.

Depth and current speed will change as you move along. Your casting angle in relation to the current must change as well. It should rarely be straight across the currents, because that angle gives maximum leverage to the current against the line, forming the greatest downstream belly, during the time you'd like your streamer to be sinking, not swinging. A cast slightly downstream, especially with some slack tossed onto the water to chase it, will sink faster than a cast that lies at a 90-degree angle across the currents.

Give your depth-charge line at least a few feet of drift to wrench the fly to the bottom. As soon as you've judged that it's there, take up any slack to gain contact with the fly. Fish it on the swing, swimming and bouncing slowly down on the bottom or just above it. Alternate a steady swing on one cast with a teasing motion of your rod tip that swims the fly a foot and rests it, swims and rests it, on the next cast. You never know which retrieve trout will want to whack. Try both to give them the choice.

Once you've worked out a comfortable length of line, casting long but without ever exceeding your grace, move downstream a step or two after fishing out each cast. Keep in constant touch with your fly so you can feel takes as soon as they happen. Some will be thuds, others no more than slow uptakes of pressure against the rod tip. You need to sense these and to rap the hook home. Then hold on. In big water, trout that take streamers are quite often whoppers.

13

Wet Flies and Wet-Fly Fishing

Our fly-fishing forefathers caught lots of trout on wet flies, fished almost entirely on a downstream swing. Now we denigrate what they did so successfully, calling it mere "chuck and chance it." We suspect wets worked then because trout were stupid, whereas now they've gotten educated by us and so are suddenly smart.

That's not true. Our predecessors knew precisely what they were doing. Wet flies worked then and work now because they resemble a lot of the natural insects trout make a living eating every day. The downstream swing was and always will be successful because it shows a wet fly, or a brace of them, to trout the same way many of those submerged naturals arrive: just tossed onto the water and washed downstream in a tangle of legs, wings, and antennae.

It's no accident that wet flies, when tied right and fished right, fool a lot of trout, including many that are far from foolish. Wet flies will never displace dry flies or nymphs from the times and places when those types of flies work best, just as those later inventions should not displace wets in situations where wets will work best.

Each of the four major fly types—dry, nymph, streamer, and wet—has its time of greatest importance. If you tie and carry a small set of wets, and learn to employ a few wet-fly methods when they're the best to set against trout, you'll increase the number of times you're able to solve an angling enigma, catch some trout, and have some fun.

Wet flies are tied in three styles: traditional winged wets, wingless wets or flymphs, and soft-hackled wets. Each has its own origins, a separate focal point, or feature of most importance, and a specific place in the repertoire of fly-fishing methods.

The traditional winged wet originated in the days of Izaak Walton and Charles Cotton and even earlier. Wets were likely the first of all trout flies. It's easy to see them in Dame Juliana Berners's descriptions of her twelve flies, in the earliest existing angling writing, *Treatyse of Fysshynge with an Angle*, published in 1496.

Early wet flies were tied as imitations of adult insects sitting at rest on streamside sticks, stones, and grasses. Anglers observed trout eating mayflies, caddisflies, and stoneflies as these emerged from the water. They captured them at rest and copied them in that posture with the materials available at the time. They fixed their flies to horsehair leaders in gangs of three or more, dapped and danced them downstream on lines a little longer than their long, stout rods. Trout sometimes took the flies as they dangled on top, but most of the time they took them submerged.

The focal point of the winged wet is the wing itself. It was and still is nearly always tied of stiff sections cut from paired mallard, goose, or pheasant wing flight feathers. Such wet flies are excellent representations of adult insects at rest in streamside vegetation. But it's better to tie your winged wets as representations of the same insects drowned and beneath the surface of the water.

To do this, reduce the wing's bulk and use softer wing materials, such as snipe, starling, and teal wing, which will tatter quickly when you get them wet. They won't be as pretty, especially after you've fished them a bit. But a wing of stiff quill cleaves the water like the blade of a knife, acts like a rudder and steers the fly around, or if it's not mounted perfectly straight, causes the fly to spiral through the water on the retrieve. Insects do not do that.

In recent years, I've been experimenting with wings of bunched hen hackle fibers rather than quill. Not all of the results are in, but trout have expressed mild approval. A hen hackle wing is far easier to tie than quill, and it works more vibrantly in the water.

You can also improve traditional winged wets by tying them with fibrous fur bodies that also work in the water, rather than yarn or floss. A body with lots of loose hairs sticking out makes the fly look alive. Don't wind dubbing onto the hook tightly. Twirl a spiky dubbing rope instead. Make sure the body is a working part of every winged wet you tie.

The final step in tying an effective winged wet fly is to palmer the hackle over the front third to half of the fly body. Hackle represents the legs, antennae, and wings of a natural. These do not arise from a single point behind the insect's head, as wet-fly hackle is normally wrapped in several turns right behind the hook eye. Instead, wind your hackle in three to four turns spaced over the front part of the fly. The traditional winged wet fly tied this way will look far more alive when wet and in the water.

Pete Hidy, coauthor with James Leisenring of the classic *The Art of Tying the Wet Fly*, coined the term flymph for wingless wet flies. To him, an insect emerging inches beneath the surface was "not yet a fly, but no longer a nymph," so Hidy declared imitations of this intermediate stage flymphs.

The earliest illustrated wingless wet flies are W. C. Stewart's spiders, from his 1857 book *The Practical Angler*. The hackle on his spider is spread over the front half of the hook. If you were to wind the same hackle all at the hook eye rather than spreading it, a spider would look like today's soft-hackled wet fly, of which it is almost certainly the ancestor. Stewart's spider is likely the root that split and evolved into both the wingless wet and the soft-hackled wet fly.

Leisenring and Hidy's book was the first American work to model wet flies on natural insects. Almost all of the flies in the book are wingless wets. The focal point is the body. Fur dubbing, usually with some guard hairs left in, is spread crosswise on sticky waxed thread, then twisted together in a thread loop to form a fur rope, out of which the body is wound. The resulting body is at once durable, buggy, and fibrous. It looks and acts lifelike in the water.

A desired undercolor is captured inside the fur body when you choose the correct color of Pearsall's Gossamer silk for tying thread. Most emerging insects have an outer and an inner color that are different. The thin outer skin of a mature mayfly nymph contains the fully formed mayfly dun, almost always a different color. The caddis pupal exoskeleton holds the caddis adult, again not often the same color as the pupa that contains it. The fur for the flymph body should reflect the outer color of the insect. The silk on which the dubbing rope is twisted should represent the inner color. When the fly is wet, these two colors will both be revealed subtly to trout about to take the fly.

To make a flymph look even more natural and alive, palmer the hackle over the front third to half of the body, the same as you just learned to do it on a traditional winged wet. This makes it look and act more like a natural insect, either emerging or drowned.

The resurrection of the soft-hackled wet fly in America can be traced directly to the 1975 publication of Sylvester Nemes's *The Soft-Hackled Fly*. Soft-hackles have their origins in the same border region between Scotland and northern England where W. C. Stewart fished his slightly earlier spiders. Thrifty Scots tied flies that reflected their spare lives. The flies had a body of tying silk and a turn or two of hackle from some found feather. That's all. The hackles were soft, which improved them, because the fibers of such feathers move well in the water.

The focal point of the soft-hackled wet fly is its hackle. The body is thin, usually no more than a couple layers of tying silk. A small fur thorax, just a few turns of dubbing wound behind the hackle, serves to prop the hackle up and make it move more in the water. The hackle collapsing around the silk body and thorax constitutes the body of the fly when it's fished. The silk body then becomes the important undercolor. Stray fibers of hackle that open and close in the current represent the appendages of a battered insect.

Soft-hackled wets can represent the drowned adult stage of three major aquatic insect orders: mayflies, caddisflies, and stoneflies. They also imitate the pupal stage of the caddis, sometimes dashing, at other times rising slowly to the surface with legs and antennae trailing. To tie effective soft-hackle imitations of these disorganized insects, keep the hackle sparse, two to at most three turns of partridge, starling, snipe, or some other soft feather.

Fishing methods used to present wet flies to trout are at least as important as the techniques used to tie them. If you fish the right fly the wrong way, not much will happen. Show trout a wet fly that is slightly wrong, but with a presentation that fishes it as if it's alive, and they'll often accept it no matter how it's tied.

The upstream wet-fly method fishes the submerged fly just like a dry fly, but inches deep rather than afloat. The purpose of the method is to present the wet fly on a dead drift, without any action at all. It works best on smooth to slightly riffled water, during a hatch, when trout feed steadily but take insects just subsurface rather than right on top. Switch to a wet if all of your attempts with dry flies fail.

Equipment for the upstream wet-fly method is precisely what you're using when you decide it's time to switch from a dry. Just nip off the dry and tie on the wet. The best fly will be a flymph or soft-hackle the size and color of the adult insect you're seeing in the air or on the water.

Position yourself and present the wet exactly as you would a dry fly in the same situation. Move within 40 feet or less of the water you want to fish. The closer you get, the better you'll be able to notice the subtle signs of takes. Make your cast at an angle that cuts across the current from 30 to 60 degrees. If you cast straight upstream, you'll line the fish and spook it, just as you would when fishing a dry fly.

Control of the drift consists merely of drawing in slack line as the sunk fly moves downstream toward your position, so you can set the hook when a trout takes the fly. With a wet, you'll rarely see that take. Watch for a slight dart of the line tip, or a sudden submergence of the leader where it enters the water. At times you'll see a wink in the water where you suspect your fly to be. If you do, raise the rod to set the hook. That's a trout intercepting your drifting wet fly.

The Nemes Mended Swing is a refinement of the standard down-and-across swing that we mistakenly call "chuck and chance it." The old method was remodeled modestly by soft-hackle guru Sylvester Nemes.

Nemes's method has two purposes. The first is to explore all the water down a long riffle or slightly troubled and shallow run: the kind of water where trout might hold anywhere along the bottom but are always near enough to the surface to rise up and attack a shallow wet. The second purpose of the method is to show a soft-hackled wet, traditional wet, or a pair of them on a slow and lazy swim through a pod of rising trout in any kind of water. It works best if those trout are feeding on caddis pupae rising toward the top. Evidence of this is a scattering of adult caddis in the air but a lack of success when you try dry flies that match them. Try a traditional winged wet fly or soft-hackle whenever caddis are on the wing but trout refuse your dry flies.

Equipment for the Nemes Mended Swing is the same as that for most other wet-fly methods: a floating line and a leader slightly longer than the rod you're fishing. If you choose to use a pair of flies, try two that are substantially different: one large and one small, one bright and one dark, or one soft-hackle and one winged or wingless wet. You can add the dropper fly by tying it to an uncut tag of the tippet knot. You can also tie a 2-foot tippet to the hook bend of the first fly, and tie a new point fly at the end of this extended tippet.

Take your position at the top end of the riffle or run you're about to fish. If you're casting over a pod of rising trout, move to a position upstream and off to the side at a 45- to 60-degree angle. In either case, your cast should cut downstream and across the current and be no longer than 40 to 50 feet, unless it's impossible to wade nearer to the water you want to fish.

When the cast lands, you must control the angle at which the line lies across the current, which affects the speed at which the fly swims through its swing. If the line begins to belly downstream and speeds the fly, toss upstream mends to remove the belly. Whenever the fly begins to swim faster than a natural insect might, make upstream mends to slow it. I've watched Nemes fishing his own method. He makes nearly constant mends from the time the fly lands until it swings straight below him and stops . . . or is tapped at by a trout.

The Hidy Subsurface Swing is designed to take trout feeding selectively and specifically on that stage of the insect for which the term flymph originated: aquatic insects emerging just beneath the surface, then struggling to the top with wings and legs and antennae all awash. But it works as well in the hour or so after a mayfly hatch, when lots of duns drift along drowned just beneath the surface.

I've also had exceptional luck with the method when caddis adults dive to the bottom to lay their eggs. The two most common stream caddis types, gray sedges and spotted sedges, both exhibit this behavior, and trout take advantage of it often. When they do, you see many caddis adults in the air and lots of rises on the water. These look like surface takes, but they're usually scant inches deep. Go ahead and try the dry fly; I do too. But when it fails, which it often though not always will, switch to a flymph or winged wet the size and color of the adults, and present it with the Hidy Subsurface Swing.

Equipment for the method is the same floating line, long leader, and fine tippet you were using when you tried the dry. Tie on the wet fly and you're ready to fish. Take a position upstream and off to the side from a single rising trout or from a pod of them. Cast downstream and across to the trout, placing the fly about 2 feet upstream and 3 to 5 feet beyond the trout's position.

When the fly lands, all those spiky body and hackle fibers will prevent it from sinking. Give it a sharp tug to draw it beneath the surface. Then simply follow the swing with your rod and let the current escort the fly right in front of the trout's nose. The water will bulge up, and you'll feel a rap. Don't yank to set the hook. It's already set anyway. Jerk and you'll just break off a trout of any size.

If you're fishing a pod of rising trout with the Hidy Subsurface Swing, always single out a fish and present the fly across its bow. If that trout fails to take on the first swing, don't lift the fly to present it again. Instead, let it swing slowly through the entire pod. In this manner, it will show itself to trout after trout, some of which will try to eat it.

The greased line method was devised by A. H. E. Wood and detailed in Jock Scott's *Greased Line Fishing for Atlantic Salmon*. It was worked out for presenting a salmonfly broadside down the current, as if it were a freely drifting leaf, with no influence from the line and leader. The method is useful on trout, for fishing winged wets, flymphs, or soft-hackles on riffled or briskly flowing water during a mayfly hatch, when lots of duns are drowned and drifting at the whim of the currents. You won't use the method often, but you'll be glad you know how to do it when you need it.

Equipment is again just what you'd use to fish a dry fly on the same water: a floating double-taper line for increased mending ability, an 8- to 10-foot leader, and a wet fly approximately the size and color of the naturals you see on the water or in the air.

Take up your casting position straight across from the water you want to fish. Make your cast slightly upstream from straight across. Follow with immediate and constant upstream mends to keep the current from pushing a downstream belly into the line. As long as the line is relatively straight to the fly, there will be no downstream draw, and the fly will drift freely, broadside to the current and at the same speed.

Detecting takes with the greased line method would seemingly be difficult, because you're fishing a line that's not tight. In my experience, trout take with an upstream surge so certain that the line is drawn tight and a thump is felt. Raise the rod gently to set the hook, and you'll prod a trout into dancing in the air.

Once you've mastered tying the three styles of wet flies—the traditional winged wet, flymph, and soft-hackle—it takes a surprisingly simple set of tactics to fish them effectively. The upstream wet-fly method, the Nemes Mended Swing, the Hidy Subsurface Swing, and the greased line method enable you to present the three separate styles of wet flies in an appropriate manner to solve some angling situations in which dry flies, nymphs, and streamers all fail to take trout.

Sometimes these will be selective situations, in which trout feed on a specific stage of a single species of insect. Solving such a difficulty with wet flies, especially if they're presented on the traditional downstream wet-fly swing, will make you happy and will give your fly-fishing forefathers some relief in their long rest. Neither they nor their trout were nearly so foolish as we thought.

14

Soft-Hackle Success

One of the simplest and at the same time most pleasant ways to consistently make contact with trout is to swing a soft-hackled wet fly through the kind of water where trout hang out most of the time: bumpy riffles and broken runs. This is especially true in mid to late summer, when a wide variety of caddis species are busy rushing toward the top, as pupae, to make their emergence as adults, or diving down toward the bottom, as adults, to lay the eggs of the next caddis generation.

It's no secret that Sylvester Nemes is one of my heroes. Sylvester did not invent soft-hackled wets, but his book *The Soft-Hackled Fly* brought them to American attention, resurrecting work begun in 1857 when W. C. Stewart wrote about his spiders in *The Practical Angler*, published in Great Britain but now long out of print, and continued in T. E. Pritt's *Yorkshire Trout Flies*, published in Britain in 1885 and portions of which are reproduced in Nemes's *Soft-Hackled Fly Addict*.

When Sylvester's small but persuasive book arrived, I was struck by the simplicity of the flies and of the methods he described to fish them. I immediately assigned a tiny fly box to them and tied a narrow assortment, just a half dozen each of a half dozen patterns, to fill it. That happy activity—they're so pretty and alive-looking with their speckled partridge hackles—took little more than a long evening.

I fished the flies the next time I was out on water and enjoyed some minor success with them. I was not astounded by it, but I had enough fun, and caught enough trout, to review Sylvester's new book in a magazine. I recommended that everybody read it for the pleasure of the prose, tie a few of the flies for the pleasantness of their prettiness, and fish them for the few trout they might add to the average catch. That review brought me a letter from Syl that contained appreciation, but also a mild scolding for not reporting that soft-hackled flies catch both lots of trout and large trout. We began to correspond, eventually fished together, and I then learned that they indeed can catch lots of trout.

The water was the Yellowstone River, above Livingston, Montana, during the Mother's Day caddis hatch, a size 16 species in the American Grannom group (Brachycentridae). It comes off in early spring but has counterpart species that hatch in summer and continue through all of fall. Now here's the first bit of concrete advice in this piece: Whenever you fish with somebody you know to be an expert in a method, quell your own urge to catch fish, sneak around, and watch him catch his. I went some way downstream from Syl, where I think he thought I was out of sight, then sat on a bankside boulder and spied on him with the little binoculars that I always carry while I'm fishing—that's a second and accidental bit of advice: carry binoculars, whether for spying on better anglers or for peering into the feeding lanes of rising trout without the need to wade in and spook them to see what they're taking.

Sylvester fished his Mother's Day Caddis Soft-Hackle. The water where he cast was broad, more than 100 yards across, but the caddis—and as a consequence, the trout—concentrated within 30 feet of the bouldered banks. Lots of adult insects boated on the surface, and lots of noses poked out to take them. "It looks like you should fish a dry," Syl told me before I sneaked off, "but more trout are feeding on rising pupae and drowned adults just beneath the surface. And if you fish a dry, it's hard to spot it among all the naturals. You never know when you get a hit. With a wet, you always feel the take."

At first, as I watched Syl fish, it looked like he did no more than cast his fly out across the current, then let it swing down and around. At times, when the speed and shape of the currents were correct, that was precisely all he did. Life was as simple as that. It was the old wet-fly swing. And he did catch lots of trout. But as I watched longer, and as Syl moved downstream along the bank into water where the currents began to be shaped differently, I began to notice a couple minor complexities that added to his success. I think I'll back away from Sylvester, leave him alone next to the bank there, enjoying himself entertaining all those trout, in order to broaden this piece from the Yellowstone to include all of the waters that you fish as well.

The first change that Syl worked in his fishing was to vary the angle of his cast, out across the current, according to the speed at which the current swept past him. You should do the same thing whenever you fish any kind of wet fly, or even a nymph on the swing, on any size and kind of water. Here is the formula, all condensed: The slower the water flows, the higher into the current you cast, for a longer and therefore faster swing of the fly. But that might be putting it backward, so let me elongate and more fully explain the formula.

When you cast at an angle downstream and across a current, the current tugs on the fat line more than it does on the thin line tip and leader, therefore creating a downstream curve, called a *belly*, which causes the fly to race, like the tip of a drover's whip. Your fly in the water will rarely break the speed of sound, but it will commonly get going too fast for trout to believe it's any kind of natural food form. To compensate for this bellying effect, if the current is flowing fast, you cast at an angle farther downstream. This reduces the bite of the current on the line, keeps the belly to a minimum, and slows the swing of the fly. Naturally, if you cast farther downstream and not so far out into the current, you also reduce the distance the fly swings across the current. When the fly moves at the right speed, however, you increase the number of trout you catch even though you reduce the distance the fly swims.

To follow the formula out: As the current slows, you cast higher into it and farther out across it to increase the line belly, and therefore the speed of the soft-hackle swing. The slower the water you're fishing, the more nearly you cast straight across it.

Let me try to add some angles to the formula, though I don't believe that trout fishing can be reduced to geometry, so they're only approximate. When you get onto actual water, you're going to have to do this by feel. Let's say you're standing on one bank, and that bank is the baseline. A cast aimed directly at the far bank would then be at a 90-degree angle. Most of your wet-fly casts, on the average run of trout stream currents, will be made between 30 and 60 degrees downstream. If you've followed my logic—I won't blame you if you haven't; I didn't do well in geometry, either—you would typically cast at a 30-degree angle in fast water, a 45-degree angle in moderate water, and a 60-degree angle in slow water. Your soft-hackle would then achieve about the right speed in each piece of water.

After you've chosen the correct angle for the cast, based on the speed of the current, you have one very minor complexity to add, and it will come as no news. You mend the line to adjust the speed of the fly while it is making its swing, trying to entice trout for you. You already know how to do that. If you notice that the belly in the line has increased into too great a downstream curve, and sense that the fly is beginning to swing too fast, you make a brisk outward and upward thrust of your rod tip, picking up as much of the line belly off the water as possible, rolling it over in the air and back onto the water in an upstream belly. This instantly slows the fly. The current must push the line back into a downstream belly before the fly begins to accelerate again.

If the current is fast, and you cast across it at a 30-degree angle, you still might need to make almost constant mends to slow the swing of the fly. If the current is moderate, and you cast across it at a 45-degree angle, you might need to make a few lazy mends to adjust the speed. If the current is slow, and you cast across it at a 60-degree angle, an occasional mend during the long duration of that teasing swing will keep the fly ambling along at the correct pace. In long pools of some of the most patient streams, I have found it useful to cast straight across the current, at a 90-degree angle, and make a *downstream* mend as soon as the fly lands. This puts a downstream belly in the line, by intention, and gives what little current exists a slight purchase on the line, causing the fly to kick up its heels into a swim that I believe to be attractive to trout. It's also nothing new. In Atlantic salmon fishing, it's called the Crosfield Draw. I've caught lots of trout using it.

I recall a brief ego boost I got once on Oregon's lower Powder River, a creeping tailwater that had trout back then, before it dried up in a long drought and its trout blew away. I was casting a soft-hackle straight across a pool, sliding it up under some willows that drooped off the far bank. After each cast, I tossed a long downstream mend, then gazed around at the scenery while the fly began its slow swim out from under those willows. Often enough, a trout happened.

After one cast and mend, I looked downstream to see a couple young fellows walking my bank. They chatted their way along, said hello to me as they passed politely behind me, continued on upstream and were almost out of sight when a trout tugged at my soft-hackle. I didn't want them to know I had one on, so I didn't lift my rod or shout or any of the normal things I do. But the trout was a fat one, close to a couple pounds. It jumped and landed with a smack. Those guys were close enough to hear it, and I was close enough to hear one of them say, "That guy sure looks like he knows what he's doing." They didn't know me as well as you do, and I was carrying a bamboo rod, which in those distant days probably would have prompted them to say the same thing had I been over there under the brush, wading up to my shoulders, thrashing my rod tip around trying to unhook an errant cast from those willows.

I have one last thing to add to the simplicity of fishing soft-hackled flies, beyond casting at the correct angle across the current and mending the line once it lands. You need to get a feel for that right speed fly swing. You need to know, as the great Sylvester puts it, "when the fly is coaxing the fish."

The right speed for a soft-hackle swing is about the same speed that a natural insect might move in the same set of currents. As I think W. C. Stewart said it, insects don't swim with the agility of otters. They do, however, have some animation, especially those caddis I mentioned, either rising as pupae or swimming down as adults to lay their eggs. So your fly should swim, but not swiftly. How do you calculate the correct speed? You don't. You get a feel for it. And, unfortunately, you don't do that by reading Syl's book or this one. You've got to tie or buy a few soft-hackles, go out and use them.

You learn the right speed soft-hackle swing, which seems to be about the same in all types of water, by catching fish and by remembering how fast your fly was traveling at the instant a fish hit and, as you continue fishing, many fish hit. But don't concentrate on trying to recall what your fly was doing before a trout took it. Just fish the flies, fiddle around with angles of the cast and degrees of mending. You'll catch fish, at first seemingly at random. When you catch them, your subconscious will record how the fly was moving when the hits occurred. Soon your hand and arm, without any direction from you, will begin casting at the right angle across all the various currents and mending the line at all the right moments.

That is another reason fishing soft-hackles is so much fun, beyond the beauty of them and the simplicity of the methods used to fish them: You learn to catch fish on them by catching fish on them.

A sample set of soft-hackled wets:

PARTRIDGE & YELLOW

Hook:	standard wet fly, size 10–16
Thread:	yellow Pearsall's Gossamer silk
Hackle:	gray partridge
Body:	2 layers of working thread
Thorax:	hare's mask fur

PARTRIDGE & GREEN

Hook:	standard wet fly, size 10–16
Thread:	green Pearsall's Gossamer silk
Hackle:	gray or brown partridge
Body:	2 layers of working thread
Thorax:	hare's mask fur

GROUSE & ORANGE

Hook:	standard wet fly, size 10–16
Thread:	orange Pearsall's Gossamer silk
Hackle:	grouse wing shoulder feather
Body:	2 layers of working thread
Thorax:	hare's mask fur

MOTHER'S DAY CADDIS

Hook:	Tiemco 900BL, size 16
Thread:	black 6/0
Body:	peacock herl
Hackle:	gray partridge, one turn, gathered over back
Head:	black mole fur

15

Poking at Pockets:
The Upstream Approach

I just got back from a trip to Oregon's famous Deschutes River. Fishing was excellent, once I found the trout and devised a way to con them into taking a fly. But that's what trout fishing almost always gets reduced to: finding fish and figuring out a way to fool them.

The Deschutes has a lot of perfect bank water. That's where I always look for trout first. But salmonflies were long gone, and no terrestrials were around yet to tempt trout to feed along the banks, so I hiked downstream from camp to the nearest riffle corner, where trout always hang out. Unfortunately, I got there a little late; three anglers were already lined up, trotting nymphs. They greeted my arrival with glowers, so I just watched them fish for a while, during which time they exercised their flies fruitlessly, which made me feel at least marginally better.

I hiked back toward camp, passing along the river, and noticed one of those long, rumpled stretches of pocket water that exist on nearly every river and are nearly always neglected by anglers. Trout fail to make that same mistake. They live there, though usually in secret and unmolested by anglers. I plunked my rear on a streamside rock and watched the water awhile. Most of it was fast and frothed: too brutal to hold fish. But boulders broke the current, bounced it back and forth, caused soft spots here and there.

A few caddisflies danced, and I noticed a couple mayflies take to the air. These scant insects were far from a hatch. But they constituted just the kind of scattered activity that prompts pocket water trout into an interest in the surface.

What got me up and interested was a splashy rise that erupted in a small soft spot behind a boulder. Before wading out and casting to it, I took time to stouten my tippet to fresh 4X, to dress three-quarters of my leader with dry-fly floatant, and to tie on a size 12 parachute pattern with a brown body and yellow wing-post. I wanted a dry fly that would float well and be visible in such rough water.

I used my wading staff to prop me into position, 20 feet directly downstream from the boulder behind which I'd seen the rise. This is one of the secrets of fishing pocket water: If you can cast short and directly upstream into the pocket, the conflicting currents off to each side will not draw your line in one direction and your leader in the other, causing drag.

On the first cast, I got drag anyway. The faster water downstream from the pocket, nearer to me, drew the line tight and began to scoot the fly. The instant it did, I rolled the fly into the air with the hope it would look to trout like an insect that had landed on the water, skidded a couple of inches, changed its mind, and lifted off. That's a second secret: Let your fly skid the length or breadth of a pocket, and you've aroused an alarm in the trout that renders further casts with that same fly largely a waste of time.

On the next cast, I overshot the pocket, then put on the brakes while the line was still in the air, so the line and leader dropped to the sweet spot with lots of slack. As soon as they touched down, I lofted the rod as high as I could to lift the line nearest me off the faster water. It worked. The fly bobbed behind the rock for a moment, then began to drift slowly downstream with no tug from the line or leader. A trout smacked it before all the slack had played out, bounded downstream, flapped into the air, ran around a rock, and snapped the tippet. I stood stunned but had gotten a good look at the trout suspended in the air. It was about 16 inches long, and fat.

It took a few minutes to fumble on another fly and return to fishing. Before I finished wading upstream, finishing out that short stretch of pocket water back to camp, I saw three more trout in the air but lost them, held four wet and dripping in my hands, and had a few boils at the fly that missed but gave me moments of excitement, which is most of what I'm after, anyway.

When you fish pocket water with dry flies, the main thing you seek in order to ignite excitement is control of the drift of your fly. The first factor in control is your approach to the pocket. It should be made from downstream or off to the side, for an upstream cast, and you should get as close as you can to that spot of soft water where it's most likely you'll find a fish. When fishing pocket water upstream, with dry flies or anything else, a 20-foot cast is normal. A 30-foot cast is a long one.

If you're able to cast straight upstream, you'll be in the best position to combat drag. Often, however, the only approach will be from one side, in which case you'll need to wade even closer, because you'll need to lift your line above the fast current skating along the outside edges of the slower pocket.

The second factor in control, after the proper approach and assumption of the best position, is the right rigging. It's simple: Use a leader the length of the rod, which should be 8½ to 9½ feet long. Make sure the tippet is stout enough to turn over the size fly you use. This adds control on the cast. It also helps you contain trout in the fast water in which you'll have to play them. If you dress the leader with floatant down to the tippet knot, the leader will skate rather than sink, reducing drag.

The third factor in control is the cast itself. Your approach dictates the distance: the shorter, the better. In pocket water, you can wade right up onto trout without alarming them, so long as you don't splash around, knock rocks together, or otherwise cause any extra commotion. It's common to catch trout by dangling the fly onto a pocket with not much more than the leader beyond the rod tip. No matter how long your cast, install some slack into it by stopping the rod while the line is in the air or by wiggling the rod as the line loop unfurls. Then lift the rod the instant the cast lands, to hold as much line as possible off the water.

The fourth and final factor in pocket water control, and often the most important, is mending and tending the drift after the fly lands on the water. If your line lies across the seam between fast water and slow, and a downstream belly forms, you can make an upstream mend or roll to prevent drag, or at least delay it. If your line lands on fast water downstream from slow water in the pocket, you can toss extra line onto the water by wobbling your rod and feeding slack to the fast current. This extends the drift of the fly. If all else fails, flip a soft roll cast upstream toward the fly. When the hoop of line collapses, the current has slack to draw out before it begins to scoot your fly along.

Be creative. Anything you can do to increase the distance and duration of the dragless drift will increase the number of trout you catch. The longer your dry fly floats freely up top, the better the chance that a trout will notice it and spear up to take it.

It's often overlooked that you need to achieve precisely the same result, when fishing pocket water with the upstream approach, in order to entice trout to a nymph down near the bottom. You need to place the fly in the pocket, then control its drift so it remains there as long as possible and moves naturally when making its eventual exit. The four factors in achieving this control remain the same: your approach, the best rigging, a careful cast, and control of the drift after the nymph lands.

The approach to pocket water, when you fish upstream with nymphs, is no different than you'd use when stalking the same pocket with a dry fly. You want to get as near as you can. If possible, take a position directly downstream from the pocket, because that delivers your drift down the most even set of currents. A 25- to 35-foot cast will work from straight downstream. If you must take a position to one side, causing your line to cut across the faster outside current while the nymph dangles in the slower pocket, then it's best if you're 10 to 20 feet from the water you desire to fish.

The best way to rig to nymph pockets is with a bright and buoyant strike indicator 3 to 6 feet up the leader from the fly. Separate the indicator and fly a distance about twice the depth of the water. Don't set them apart much more than about 6 feet, though, or they will constantly land on separate currents and therefore drift in different directions. When that happens, you'll lose the chief thing you're after: control of the drift of the fly.

You'll need weight to get the fly down quickly. If you use split shot on the leader, keep it 8 to 10 inches from the fly. I prefer to use a stoutly weighted fly. Rick Hafele, an aquatic entomologist and expert with nymphs, often rigs with a size 8 or 10 heavily weighted nymph to achieve depth and a size 14 or 16 lightly weighted nymph as an added enticement. He takes most trout on the small fly but confesses he would not catch as many as he does without the heavy fly to deliver the light one deep.

The cast is just as critical in nymphing as it is with a dry fly. The best cast will plunk the nymph into the pocket an instant before the strike indicator lands almost on top of it. That's so the nymph sinks quickly and so they both travel in the same set of currents.

To accomplish this, employ the great Joe Humphreys's tuck cast, outlined in his book *Trout Tactics*. Too briefly described (I instruct you to read his fine book), the tuck is executed by making a straight overhand cast, but stopping the rod abruptly and holding it high at the end of the power stroke. This causes the nymph to tuck in under the line tip and to land before the indicator, but in the same spot. The fly sinks with no hindrance.

The tuck cast puts you in position to carry out the final bit of negotiations with the trout: control of the drift of your nymph. As with the dry fly, be creative. Mend and tend the line. Flip it upstream or down. Lift the indicator and set it back down without disturbing the sink and then the drift of the nymph. When the indicator takes a sudden dip, lift your rod to set the hook. Sometimes it will be bottom. That means you're fishing right.

More often it will be a trout. A fish on, dashing and dancing down the fast current in a piece of pocket water, is the best indication that you've solved upstream pocket water fishing, whether you're doing it with a dry fly or nymph.

16

Poking at Pockets:
The Downstream Approach

The stream is Stu's and not mine to name, but it's just like some of the ones you fish. It has standard riffles, runs, and pools. It also has short stretches where the water bounds among boulders and forms pockets that make it difficult to wade into position to fish. They are not fished often. They hold lots of trout. I constantly get the urge to poke into these pockets. I'm never sorry when I do. But I bumped into a day when I became sorry about the way I did it.

I did it by wading straight upstream, fighting the current. I leaned against my wading staff and pushed myself into position to set a dry fly or nymph in the soft spots right behind boulders breaking the current. It was tough work, but I was rewarded with an occasional trout that smacked the fly and dashed off on a wonderful fight. I was far from unhappy. I was also never far from disaster.

A tithe of my happiness took off when I ceased my brutal wading awhile to gaze upstream at Stu Barkley, an ex-fighter pilot, jet-sticking a flock of rainbows around the head of the same patch of pocket water I fished. Stu stood off to the side of the fastest water, wading knee-deep. He cast fairly long, 45 to 50 feet. He mended and tended the drift of whatever he was using as it swung around and down through the same difficult water I fished by wading directly into the teeth of it. He stayed out of the brutal currents, letting his fly explore them for him.

Stu kept trout in the air constantly. It was such a fascinating sight that I decided to wade out, walk up, see how he did it. I was ready to tilt back from the brink of disaster, anyway.

What Stu did was elementally simple. He fished a weighted nymph with down-and-across-stream swings. But he controlled the drift of his fly in such a meticulous way that it probed into all the pockets above boulders and below them, swam through the fastest slices of current, and idled in all the soft spots between them. Stu's way of presenting his nymph from upstream rather than down escorted his fly into all of those potential pocket water lies. That's why he goosed so many trout into the air while I fought water.

Your goal, when you fish pocket water downstream with any kind of fly, is control over the drift or swim of the fly. The four aspects of control are the same as they are when you fish pockets upstream: your approach to the piece of water, the rigging you choose to fish it, the cast itself, and the mending and tending that you do after the line and fly land on the water.

When approaching pocket water from upstream, in order to fish it with a down-and-across swing, you can cast from quite a ways away, as Stu Barkley so aptly demonstrated. You don't need to get right up onto the water you're going to fish, though it won't cost anything if you do. This flexibility allows you to fish pocket water from a slight distance, therefore with some slight comfort, because you wade easier water. This is no small advantage in pocket water. It's always difficult and often dangerous.

Your angle of approach should place you upstream and across from the water where you want your fly to swim, so you can cast at an angle downstream and across the current. Try to stay within 50 feet. You'll take some trout on longer casts, but your ability to control the swing diminishes, and the odds of setting the hook successfully also drop on a longer line.

Your rigging can be kept simple. Just tie a wet fly, soft-hackle, nymph, or small streamer to the end of your leader, which should be a little longer than your rod. If you're not sure what fly to use, it's often wise to complicate things a little by using a pair of them a couple feet apart on the leader. One should be dark and one light, or try a large one chasing a small one. If you're using nymphs, one of them should be at least slightly weighted. In deep or fast pocket water, it helps if one of them is heavily weighted.

Some folks use a wet-tip line for this kind of pocket water fishing. I prefer a floating line, for two reasons. First, if trout are at all active, they'll be willing to be coaxed toward the top. Second, the submerged wet-tip does not ride up and over protruding rocks as well as a floating line. With a floater, you can toss mends or rolls just as the line bellies above a boulder, and you can usually urge it over without hanging up. Hang-ups, when you swing sunk flies downstream through pocket water, are a problem it's wise to minimize. When you fish deep and fast pockets, however, a wet-tip line can get your flies down into the strike zone and add to your catch without adding to your problems, which is a trade you should always make.

The cast is a critical element of control on the downstream swing. The angle of the cast dictates the speed of the swing. If the water is fast, cast at a sharper angle downstream, reducing line belly and slowing the swing of the fly. If the water is slow, cast higher into the current, giving the current a bit more bite on the line and spurring the fly. Pocket water is rarely lazy, so you will cast down and across a lot more often than you will straight across.

Mending and tending of the cast, once the line is on the water, should be done with two outcomes in mind. The first is to guide the fly through the pockets you want it to probe. Coax it along; tug it upstream or down, right or left, so that it swims through all of the water where you might expect trout to hold and lots of the water where you might not.

The second mission of mending and tending is to adjust the speed of the swing. Toss upstream mends in fast water to reduce a downstream belly in the line and therefore to slow the swing of the fly. I'd tell you to take downstream mends in slow water to speed the swing of the fly, but you'd get smart and say, hey, when was the last time you fished slow pocket water, Dave? More often than not, your fly will swim too fast in pocket water.

If even constant mending fails to cure it, then strip line from the reel and wobble slack onto the water beyond the rod tip. This installation of slack instantly slows the swing and drift of the fly.

Fishing a sunk fly on the swing through pocket water is highly effective, I think sometimes because it catches the trout by surprise. They don't see flies arrive that way very often anymore. Another way to surprise pocket water trout is to approach close to them, from upstream, and drop either a dry fly or nymph right onto their heads.

The best approach for this method is from upstream and at a slight angle off to one side. This approach lets you wade downstream into position, which in a truly pushy current allows you to wade water you could not fight upstream. Use a wading staff, wade as carefully and quietly as you can, and don't stop until you're just a rod length or two from the pocket you want to fish.

Rigging is easy. Use a bright and visible dry fly or a stoutly weighted nymph. If I'm using a nymph, I usually add a yarn indicator 3 to 4 feet up the leader. The indicator is used to direct the drift of the nymph as well as to mark takes. The delivery of the fly is more a dangle or a dap than an actual cast. The posture is this: One hand holds the staff, the other hand holds the rod high in the air, the rod hand forefinger clamped on the line with a loop of line dangling behind it. When a trout hits, it's going to be off and running instantly, with lots of current to fuel its flight. You want some slack to give to the trout while you get control, not of the fish, but of yourself in the awkward position into which you've gotten yourself in order to hook the fish.

Control of the drift is easy at such short range, and your options are limited, anyway. About all you can do is lift your rod to keep line off the water, and lower your rod to let the dry fly dance or the nymph drift down the pocket. This works well enough in short pockets but doesn't do so well in pockets that stretch out 20 to 30 feet below a boulder. You'd be surprised, however, at how far you can coax a dry fly or nymph into a free drift if you can get your feet set and use your line hand to feed line into the drift of the fly. If it's a nymph, the free drift of the indicator down the length of a pocket will be your best indication that the nymph is fishing correctly, a few feet deep.

I made this downstream dapping method work for me on Oregon's Deschutes not long ago. A lot of pocket water on this big and brutal river pushes right up against the bank, beneath trees. You're not allowed to fish out of a boat, so this kind of water strays into almost entire neglect. Smart folks avoid it. But good things to eat drop out of those trees all the time, so trout don't. I found myself wading down a stretch of it, grasping at overhanging tree limbs with my right hand, holding my rod out beyond the limbs with my left, trying to keep control of myself and a rod length of line.

It was precarious. The current pushed me against the upstream side of a boulder. I braced against it, held on, and flipped the rod to drop a dry fly behind the boulder, nearly in front of my knees. It bobbed there so close that when a trout came up and smote it, I was able to clearly see the size of the trout's nose. It was a little frightening. But I released that loop of slack held behind my rod hand forefinger and bought time to compose myself and get the trout onto the reel.

From there on it was dash and dance, though the trout executed all the activity because I was pinned to that boulder by the current. It took quite a while to tire the trout enough to lead it back into the same small but quiet pocket where it had held, and where it had been so surprised to see my dry fly arrive.

The trout weighed around 3 pounds. I unpinned the fly, released the fish, then unpinned myself from that boulder and let the current push me down to the next boulder and next piece of pocket water behind it. I continued to dap and dangle my fly and took two more trout of similar size, before I was forced to leave the water because it became too dangerous to wade. It was impossible to wade upstream to where I had started, so I thrashed up the bank through a patch of poison oak and rattlesnakes.

Was it worth it? I don't know. But I do know one thing: Like most pieces of productive pocket water, I'm not about to see many other folks in there, and I'm bound to see some unsophisticated trout.

17

Fishing Stairsteps

My wife and I just returned from fishing the Logan River in Utah for a few days. It's a canyoned stream, bounding briskly out of all that beauty up in the Rockies. Its trout are native cutthroat, gorgeous things and supposedly stupid. But they didn't seem to know it and were quite difficult until we solved some minor problems in fly presentation. Then they became easy.

The stream had some aspects that are a lot like yours, wherever you fish, unless it's in the flatlands. I've had to solve the same presentation problems from North Carolina to New England, throughout the Rockies, and up and down the West Coast from California to Canada. The aspects are what I call "stairsteps." The problems are what we all call "drag."

Any brisk hill stream descends in a series of steep drops followed by flat benches: drop and bench, drop and bench, just like a set of stairs except the drops and benches are not often of equal dimension. Most drops are a foot or two, most benches 10 to 30 feet long. That's on the Logan. On a tiny mountain creek, a drop might be a minor waterfall, the bench might be just as abrupt. On a large river, the drop might be a short riffle, the bench a long cast long. But the features remain the same: stairsteps. So do the solutions to the problems stairsteps present.

The first part of the solution, whether you're fishing a dry fly or nymph, is to take a position that's no more than a single drop down from the bench you're intending to fish. If you take a position two drops down, letting an extra drop intervene between you and where your line and fly will land, the fast water rushing over the lower drop will grab your line and race your fly.

Here's the simple rule: When fishing stairsteps with benches a short cast long, roughly 20 to 30 feet, fish each succeeding bench from the one directly downstream from it. If you're fishing benches a medium to long cast long, say 40 to 60 feet, fish the bottom end of each bench from the bench immediately below it, then sneak up onto the bench itself to fish its upper end.

The remaining part of the solution to stairsteps is simply to lift your rod and loft your line above the rushing water of the step down to the bench from which you're casting. Keep all of your line on the even currents of the bench where your dry fly floats or where your nymph searches the bottom. Any line that's not on those even currents must be held up off the water.

By taking up the correct position, and by carrying your line above any currents not in the even sheet you're fishing, you accomplish what you're after: a drag-free presentation, no matter what type of fly you're fishing.

Dry flies are the obvious first choice if you're fishing stairsteps and trout are willing to take them. That will be most of the time. You won't have any trouble figuring out how to rig them, so I won't tell you much about that beyond making sure you're using a fly that floats on rough water and that you can see. Rig with a leader that is in balance with the size of the fly and short enough to give you control over the drift.

What do you do on those frustrating occasions when trout refuse to rise for drys, but you know they're in there and you suspect they'd take something fished at their level? My first advice is to drop a beadhead or weighted nymph off the stern of your dry fly, making sure, of course, that the dry is big enough and floats well enough to support it. Tie 2 to 3 feet of tippet, one size finer than the tippet to your dry, to the hook bend with an improved clinch knot. Tie the nymph to the other end of this extended tippet. You're rigged.

There is no real rule on the length of the tippet to the dropped fly. If I were to make one up, it would be to use about the same length tippet between the dry and nymph as the water is deep. Just remember that your goal is to show the nymph to trout holding on the bottom, within the narrow zone—a foot or so—in which they might be willing to move up from the bottom to take it.

Continue to fish the stairsteps, when rigged with a nymph dropped off your dry, just as you would with the dry alone. If the floating fly suddenly disappears, set the hook. If for some reason you lose sight of your dry, lift your rod tip to ask what has happened out there. More often than not, the weight of a fish will answer your query.

If you don't get results on a dry and dropper, assume the trout are down there but not willing to move even that short foot off the bottom. Take the time to rerig with a strike indicator, one or two small split shot on the leader, and one or two nymphs to search right along the bottom. Start with the distance between the indicator and point fly two to three times the depth of the water. Adjust the indicator up or down to lower or lift your nymph or nymphs. If you're not quarreling with the bottom on occasion, your fly is fishing too high in the water column, and it's unlikely that this rig will get you into many quarrels with trout.

On typically brisk mountain and foothill streams, the water depth will vary constantly from step to step, and at times even from end to end of the same step. Many stairstep pools have slots and trenches where the bottom drops away a foot or more, and of course, you know that's where trout will hold. When you fish stairsteps with the split shot and indicator nymph rig, use an indicator that you can easily slide up and down the leader. That's the best way to stay in constant touch with stairstep trout.

18

A Half-Solved Mystery

We all know about the switch meadow-stream trout make to feed on hoppers, ants, and beetles in late summer and early fall. They move to stream edges and winnow what lands there. We rarely relate this to the diminishment of aquatic insect hatches, but it's true. Part of this movement toward the banks is pull, as trout are drawn by the new availability of terrestrials. Part of it is push, as trout are urged out of midwater lies by a lack of food found there after stonefly, mayfly, and caddis hatches all taper off.

It all makes sense from a biological point of view. Aquatic insect adults, especially mayflies and stoneflies, bequeath a jump on life to their next generation if they emerge, mate, and lay their eggs as soon as the high waters of spring recede. This gives their future nymphs more quiet time to grow before the waters become wild again.

If you spend any time prowling streams with grassy or brushy banks in July, August, and September, you should tie or buy a small box of terrestrial patterns in a narrow range of sizes and colors. Cast these flies right along the edges, in the water you normally walk along or even wade while casting to the water farther out. In fact, let me give you an assignment to stay out of that edge water and spend some time just watching it the next time you're out after trout in warm weather.

Sit down at lunchtime or when you need a rest, right on the bank. Approach the place you'd like to sit very slowly, stooped, and insert yourself into shade, hide behind a shrub, or disappear into the depths of tall grass. Keep an open view up or down a stretch of edge water. Now nibble at your sandwich, or rest awhile, but watch the water exactly at the edge. It's possible you'll be idle a lot shorter time than you expect.

A trout might give itself away with a sipping rise behind a rock, up under the sweeping blades of a bunchgrass clump, or back beneath some overhanging limbs and leaves. Bank trout do not often rise rhythmically, as trout feeding on hatches tend to do, simply because their food drops in less consistently than hatching insects tend to ascend. So I'll give you a second assignment: When you spot a rise, before you fumble your sandwich into the water and panic after your fly rod, watch that trout expose its position, or the pattern of its movement, with a few more rises before you cast to it.

You're being instructed by the trout here. Ending the lesson too soon by casting to the fish, even if you catch it, would be a little like shooting a college professor halfway through an excellent lecture. Hold your fire for at least a moment. You'll always learn more about what a trout is doing if you watch it awhile. The more you know about what it's doing—the way it's feeding and what it might be feeding upon—the better chance you'll have at hooking it.

You'll also discover often that a bank-sipping trout is not alone. If you're even mildly patient, you might see other trout expose themselves upstream or down from where you spotted the first. Again, there usually will be little rhythm to their rises, which is one reason you need to wait them out to spot them. The other reason is that they're usually tucked into indents in the shoreline or back beneath overhanging grasses or branches, making them difficult to see.

Sometimes you'll watch edge water for a long time and suddenly see a single detonation. That marks the death of a large insect, probably a hopper or cricket. It also marks the lie of a trout that might not rise to expose itself again until you set your size 10 or 12 imitation onto its water. In the case of a splashy rise, the lesson is over: Grab your rod and shoot the professor.

This sort of waiting and watching edge water offers rewards, not all of which need be trout, but those are the ones we're talking about here, on medium streams and large rivers, often famous ones. I learned it long ago along the banks of my home Deschutes River and have employed the wait-and-watch often on such waters as the Henrys Fork of the Snake, the Madison, the Yellowstone, and the heavily pestered Bighorn River. But I've also sat happily along the pastured banks of a few Wisconsin spring creeks—I've been threatened with mayhem if I name them—watching for sipping rises tight to the cropped grasses. The rises were always delicate on those surprisingly beautiful streams, very difficult to notice, but once spotted, they always revealed large trout.

Patient watching can even pay dividends in trout on wilderness water, where you'd least expect a slowdown to speed up your fishing.

I spent most of a week one fall backpacking and casting dry flies up a small stream that had miles of forested stretches. It took a long time before some terrestrial lessons sank into my head beneath those trees, because I was too eager to be fishing to spend time at my own assignment: sitting and watching.

The lessons were different from those found along meadow streams. I was introduced to them in an awkward way. I would fish a pool as I usually do, which means by stepping to its tail-out and casting to its head, with little success. Then I'd reel up, hike up, and fish the next pool the same way with the same result: none. Every time I arrived at the tailout of a small pool, one or two V-wakes would arrow upstream through it to the fast water at its head, which is where I normally catch most of my small-stream trout.

Those V-wakes were the pointers in a lesson the trout were trying to teach me: that they were holding on the thin tailouts and I wasn't going to catch them until I figured out how to get a fly there without spooking them. The lesson led to an idea.

I'm going to expose the idea here not as fact, but as a theory. Here it is: Small-stream trout in spring and early summer, when aquatic insect hatches are healthy, hang out toward the heads of pools because that's where most of their food gets delivered. The same small-stream trout, turning to terrestrials in late summer and early fall, hang out toward the lower edges and the tailouts of forested pools because that's where they get the best line of sight on the plopping arrival of most of their food at that time of year, so they can race to get to it first.

Aquatic insects swim to the surface, hatch, and are delivered down the current. Trout get fed best on aquatics where currents gather, are briskest and most constricted: in the current tongue at the head of a pool. Terrestrial insects drop onto overshadowed pools anywhere across the broader surfaces of them. Trout get fed best on terrestrials, in small streams, where they can witness this windfall and rush forward to greet the new arrivals: lower in the pools and on the tailouts.

Both types of small-stream feeding—at the upper ends of pools in spring and early summer, at the lower ends of pools in late summer and early fall—are prompted by the same instinct and serve the same survival purpose: to be first to food. If my theory is correct, then this is one of the most observable instances I've seen of natural selection at work. It is also a visible clinic on the balance a trout must strike between the need to compete for food and its willingness to take an increased risk to satisfy it. Those trout hanging on thin tailouts were exposed to all sorts of predation from which they would have had more protection buried deep beneath the frothed current tongue entering into the head of the same pool.

I was among the predators from whom they assumed some extra risk by exposing their positions, but it took me quite a while to figure that out.

During those days spent fishing that small forested stream, I developed my theory and tested it by fishing hectically and fruitlessly at first, noticing those V-wakes but not knowing what to do about them, then finally by settling down and watching the water, after which I began to figure things out and catch some trout. The first thing I noticed during the hectic part of my careen up the stream was the holding pattern of the trout. They were not scattered in riffles, runs, and brief plunge pools where they're easy to find and also easy to catch in spring and early summer. Instead, they were scattered in the longest and broad-est and flattest pools, even if those pools were so thin that they had no depths at all.

In a pool 20 feet long—a large one on this small stream—I might cause three or four trout to arrow ahead of my clumsy approach. In a pool 40 feet long, half a dozen of them might dash off, and I might even catch one or two of them up toward the head of the pool by giving them time to settle for a while. It was that need to rest pools for a bit before casting to the trout I'd already spooked that made me think about taking some extra time on my approach, perhaps to cast to them before I spooked them rather than after.

After I wised up, sat down, and watched a few pools before splashing awkwardly up to them in my usual way, I began to solve the problem of those trout holding on small-stream tailouts in late summer and early fall. The first part of the solution will come as no surprise to you: I made a more cautious approach to the lower end of each pool and cast more carefully. The success of this simple maneuver came as a slight surprise to me because I'd always caught small-stream trout at the heads of pools, which reflects my penchant for fishing small streams early in the sea-son, then switching to larger streams and rivers later in the year. When trout hold consistently at the heads of pools, you don't spook many of them by marching proudly past the tailout.

When I began creeping up to the thin water and placing my casts so that only the line tip and leader landed on the water, those V-wakes arrowed abruptly to take my flies, not flee from them, about half the time. The other half, because of some mis-take in my approach or the clumsy arrival of my cast or some inherent invincibility in the trout's position so I could not get a cast over it without spooking it, still sent the trout shooting up the pool.

To solve that last half of the problem, I was forced to sit and watch and think some more. It finally occurred to me that the tailouts of lots of pools were simply too thin and too exposed to approach from downstream. So I crept around to the heads of these pools, kept my profile as low as possible, cast sidearm where the law of the encroaching limb allowed it, and fished my drys with downstream slack-line casts. I wiggled the rod, tossed slack, sent weak roll casts looping out halfway to the fly—did everything possible to extend the drift of the fly downstream toward those skittish trout on the thin tailouts.

It worked well enough. I caught a few of the trout I'd spooked before. But I'd get only one shot per pool. If no trout rushed up and took the fly on the first downstream float, I'd have to lift the line off the water for a second attempt. Without exception, that sent panicked arrows shooting in all directions in those small pools. That would be that.

I learned something even from that, though, and what I learned strengthened my belief in my theory about trout holding in the lower parts of pools to intercept terrestrials in late summer and early fall. It did not prove my theory but did make me feel more convinced about the likely truth of it.

That's about where I like to leave a theory and the problem to which it's attached: convinced that I've come closer to figuring things out, while those remaining spooked fish remind me that I've got a lot left to puzzle out on the next trip.

We always need reasons for next trips. Half-solved mysteries are part of what prompt them.

19

Stillwater Strategy

Lakes appear to be mysteries when you first fish them for trout. All of the surface looks the same, at least at a glance and before you know precisely what to look for. Features that tell you where trout would hold, and what foods they might be eating, are usually hidden in the depths. That is why most people enjoy fishing streams as opposed to lakes: Moving water shapes itself visibly as it flows over riffle rocks, around protruding boulders in runs, through bends to form pools, undercut banks, and other types of lies.

It seems easier to see just where trout might hold in moving water, and it also seems easier to figure out how to catch them. Not all is always as it seems.

Stillwaters are no more difficult to understand than streams if you realize there are just four things you must solve to find trout and catch them with flies. The first is the area in the lake where trout concentrate. The second is selecting the right fly to fool them. The third is using the right tackle to fish that fly at the correct depth. The fourth and final thing to solve when fishing a lake is how to present the chosen fly with the right retrieve so trout mistake it for something good to eat.

When you solve each of these four pieces of the stillwater fishing puzzle, lakes and ponds suddenly become easy. The key is to solve them one at a time, so that you do not become confused by the apparent mystery that is the surface of a stillwater.

The fastest way to find fish in a lake, and the one you should always exercise first, is to look for rises. This sounds elementary, but even experienced fishermen often forget to do it. I'll give you an example that reflects poorly on me and my choice of friends.

Some friends I'll not name and I once hiked an hour into a middle-size lake in the Cascade Mountains of Oregon. The lake was beautiful, with tall forest around most of it, a long slide of rocks along one side rising up to a ridge just above the lake. The view from that ridge looked down over the lake in one direction and out onto a lot of Oregon in the other.

My friends and I were interested in catching trout, not looking at views. We rushed to the edge of the lake, inflated our float tubes, strung our fly rods, instantly kicked out, and began casting. A quick glance at the lake surface where we'd launched revealed no rising trout, so we strung sinking lines to fish nymphs and streamers deep. It was late spring. We thought the trout might be starting to sink into the depths because the water was beginning to warm toward summer thermal layering. That was a big mistake.

We kicked around within 100 yards of shore at first, casting or towing our deep flies. After an hour of that, we all headed out and began fishing even deeper water. After a couple more futile hours spent exploring the depths, we bumped together in the center of the lake. We'd been fishing water so deep that no trout had been down there since the middle of last winter. We talked awhile, trying to decide where all the trout might be hanging out. Nobody had an answer. Everybody went in a different direction after that, and all of us tried different desperation methods. Nothing worked.

I decided to have a hike up to that ridgetop for the view, since I couldn't catch any trout. I took the little pair of binoculars that I carry whenever I'm fishing. They've accounted for nearly as many trout as my favorite fly rod, and this time was not an exception.

When I reached the top of the ridge, I relaxed and gazed out into the distance: at mountains with snow on top and mile after mile of dark conifer forest. It was beautiful. It was a long time before I turned the binoculars from the distant view to spy on my friends fishing the lake laid out below me.

It was fun to watch them kicking around in their brightly colored tubes in the sunshine, all going in different directions, all either trolling placidly or casting and retrieving frantically, trying to find the trout, catching nothing. I'll admit I'd have been distressed to climb that ridge, look back down, see someone playing a fish. I'd have had to rush down there, go at it again; you know how that goes. But they weren't catching anything, which made me happy to have the altitude I'd gained.

Then I shifted the binoculars to look around the entire lakeshore. My gaze entered a cove separated by a timbered point of land from where we had launched and where my own float tube now sat abandoned on shore. We had glanced into that shallow backwater on our way out to the depths but did not paddle in and explore it because of our hurry to move out to where we thought the big ones would be. I was surprised to notice the rise rings of several trout in the cove.

I nearly broke a leg in my hurry to get down the rock slide and back to my tube. I changed from the sinking line I'd been using to a floating line. I fumbled into my waders, jumped into my tube, and almost tipped over in getting launched. I kicked around the point, slowed and crept to where the trout still rose, and saw thousands of mayfly spinners dancing up and down in the air, just above the water, and plenty of them on it. I found a dry fly in my boxes that matched them nearly enough, tied it on, cast to the nearest trout, and set the hook when it came up with a confident rise.

The fish jumped and jumped. It was a fat rainbow, about 16 inches long. I was so excited to catch one that I accidentally let out a shout. My friends all heard it and hurried over, switched lines or switched rods if they were smart enough to have armed themselves with extras, and all began catching trout. That was a disappointment. I had hoped they would continue to have bad luck, so that I would have more to brag about later by comparison. It's not my lot very often to be the one to solve a situation.

Always take time to look carefully for rising trout as soon as you arrive at any lake, before you rig, before you begin fishing. Get to high ground if there is any, in order to see as much water as possible. I don't know how many times I've looked out over a lake from shore with my binoculars before fishing it, spotted rising trout, then launched my tube or small boat and gone at once to the best fishing possible.

Looking for rises is the first way to read a lake and find fish. There is a great advantage to finding them this way: When you do, they're already feeding, so you know they're willing to take a fly if you tie on the right one.

When no trout can be seen rising, the next place to look is around the shoreline. Trout in stillwaters are a little like bass. They hide in shade, around lily pads, wherever logs have fallen into the water, and where rocky points drop off toward deep water. These places give them shelter from their own predators and let them hide from the things that they like to ambush and eat. If I do not see rising trout on first examining a lake, I always set off fishing along the shoreline, casting to any kind of cover that looks like it might hold fish.

It is important to fish carefully where any stream enters or exits a lake or pond. Streams coming in bring cool water and also deliver both aquatic and terrestrial insect life. These attract trout. Fish also gather at entering streams before swimming up to spawn. A stream flowing out of a lake gathers foods that have emerged from the water or fallen to the surface, funneling it all down from a broad area to a narrow and moving conveyor belt. Trout wait at outlets for the gathering current to deliver this abundance to them.

If you do not find trout around the shoreline or gathered at streams flowing into or out of a stillwater, look for them around two kinds of areas farther from shore. The first is a dropoff, where the lake suddenly slides from shoreline shallows to deeper water. The second is any weed bed you can see by peering down into the water or discover by probing with your anchor. Aquatic insects and crustaceans, especially scuds, live in weed beds. Because trout eat insects and scuds, they spend a lot of time near aquatic vegetation, cruising and looking for food.

I fished a big lake in British Columbia once with Al Buhr, the famous steelhead fisherman who helps design and test two-handed rods for Sage. Al also knows trout. The lake we fished was 15 miles wide. The first morning, Al woke early and paddled out slowly from camp while standing in his canoe, watching down into the water. None of the rest of us had time for that. We went fishing, pestering the water right in front of our tents, catching a few but none that caused any of us to holler.

Al followed the shoreline around from camp until he found a place where shallow water extended far out into the lake. He followed the shallows out, still peering down, until the water suddenly dropped off into dark depths. Al eased his anchor onto the shallow side of that brink. Then he cast far out over the depths with a fast-sinking line, let the fly sink for a long time, and began retrieving it slowly back up the sloped bottom toward where he had anchored. The line stopped. Something tugged. Al tugged back. A Kamloops rainbow shot up from the deep water and high into the air. The trout weighed about 5 pounds, or so Al told us when he returned to camp for a late breakfast.

The next morning, we all went out early, right to where Al told us he'd been the day before. We found the dropoff easily enough, anchored our canoes at the edge of it, cast long, retrieved slowly just as instructed, and found lots to shout about, proving that Al, who was off exploring new water, had not been lying.

Sometimes you can spot dropoffs from a height above a lake. The aspect of the lake is a light color where it is shallow, darker where it is deeper. If you can hike high while the surface is calm, you can often see the line between light and dark that marks a dropoff stretching far out into the lake. That's the place to fish. Trout will cruise all along it, sometimes shallow, other times deeper, but always looking for insects and baitfish that live at that edge.

Weed beds always have trout cruising around, nosing in and out, eating mayfly nymphs, midge larvae, leeches, scuds, everything in their watery world that doesn't eat them. Sometimes you can find weed beds by looking over the edge of your float tube or boat. Get your face close to the water and shield your eyes with your hands to block out sunlight. That helps you see deeper. If the water is too deep to see weed beds, drop your anchor to the bottom, pull it along for a few feet, and bring it up. If it comes up with weeds on it, you've found a great place to fish. If it comes up clean, move on and look for better water.

On some sunny days, when the light strikes into the water just right, weed beds show on the surface of a lake as dark patches, especially if the lake has a light-colored bottom. These patches look like the shadows of small clouds or trees along the bank. If you ever notice such a dark spot, move over it and look into the water, or drop your anchor onto it and bring up a sample of whatever is down there. If it's weeds, or even just a dark, rocky bottom, trout will usually be there.

My father and I once fished a small, shallow lake on a bright, sunny day. The lake surface was patchy with dark spots that we did not pay attention to for some time, mistaking them for the shadows of all the tall trees cramped around the shore. We cast at random and caught fish here and there but never consistently. Then I drifted over a dark spot in my tiny boat, looked down, and realized it was a weed bed on the bottom, 10 feet deep, not the shadows of any nearby trees.

I backed off and anchored near the weed bed, fiddled with my gear to let the water settle a little, then cast over it with the sinking-tip line I already had on, since the trout I'd been catching were at about the depths of those weed tops. I let the fly sink for some time and fetched up a nice trout. I made the same cast and caught another just like it.

Dad and I began anchoring our boats a few feet away from those scattered dark areas on the bottom, then casting alongside them and over them so that our flies, when retrieved, could be seen by trout feeding in and around the weeds. We'd catch two or three trout at each anchoring, then move to another weed bed and enjoy doing it again. We caught lots of fish. All of them came from the dark parts of the bottom, none from the light-colored parts that were sandy bottom between the weed beds.

Trout drop into deep water when lakes become hot and the water stratifies in mid to late summer. They also hold deep when the water is cold in winter. In the seasons when it's most pleasant to fish lakes—spring, early summer, and again in fall—trout are not in the depths but in shallower water, because that is where sunlight strikes to the bottom, vegetation grows, insects gather, and trout come to feed on the insects.

When lakes stratify, you can find trout at times by trolling or random-casting over the depths with fast-sinking lines. But that's when I turn willingly to fishing streams instead of still-waters, because streams begin to be at their best then, and lakes are not nearly so much fun. Each thing in its season.

Many of the foods that trout eat in lakes are different from the things that they eat in streams. If you fish a lake with the same flies that work for you in moving water, you'll catch a few trout, but you won't catch as many as you could, because your flies do not look like anything the trout have eaten lately. A small knowledge of lake food forms and the flies that imitate them will help you catch more trout from lakes.

Mayfly nymphs that live in lakes are almost all swimmers. They dart about in weed beds and along the bottom, not at all like the crawlers and clingers and burrowers that hide in the gravel and silt bottoms of streams. These lake mayfly nymphs are long, slender, and have three fringed tails that serve as swimming paddles.

Because they live by eating plant growth, the bottoms and vegetation where swimmer mayfly nymphs live are almost always some shade of green. The insects must be about the same color, for camouflage, or trout would eat them all and they would become extinct. So they are almost always some shade of tannish green to dark brownish green.

The best fly patterns to match them are the Olive Hare's Ear and the Flashback Pheasant Tail, both tied on 2X long hooks in sizes 10 through 14, slightly weighted. Fish them near the bottom or alongside weed beds on a slow, twitching retrieve. Pause often in the retrieve to let them simply sit and sink, as if the natural were resting.

Mayfly duns must rest on the surface for some moments, while their wings dry, before they can fly. Trout take more may-flies as nymphs, but when duns are on the surface, trout take them often, and it's a good chance to fish lakes with dry flies over rising trout. Most lake mayfly duns the world over are brown, gray, or pale yellow on the back but a lighter shade on the bottom, usually with some green added in the mix of colors.

Because trout will be selective when these mayflies hatch, you must collect a specimen and be sure that the color of your imitation is approximately the same. I have used Harrop Hair-wing Duns and Compara-duns with olive bodies and natural grayish brown deer-hair wings all over the world, in sizes 12 and 14, but you are smarter than I am if you always collect a specimen and be sure the body color of your fly is right.

Mayfly spinners fall to the water with their wings spread flat in the surface film. The best patterns for them are A. K. Best Quill-Bodied Spinners with split hackle fiber tails, bodies of hackle stem dyed gray or reddish brown, and spent wings of grizzly hackle trimmed from the top and bottom.

Caddisflies are not often important on lakes, but when trout feed on them, you must match them or you won't catch many trout. The larvae are not important. They build cases of vegetation and crawl awkwardly in the same vegetation. Trout eat them, but not often selectively. An Olive Woolly Bugger fished very slowly will catch fish when they do.

Caddis pupae leave the cases on the bottom and rush to the surface quickly. Trout feeding on them dart out of schools, take the ascending insects with a quick turn, swim back to the school, and continue to cruise. You cannot know this is happening unless the water is so clear and the surface so calm that you can see trout swimming and feeding. There is a way to take advantage of this caddis behavior, however, without even seeing it happen.

If you see caddis adults in the air over the lake and even on the surface, but few fish are taking them, then you can be sure that the trout are feeding on the pupae coming up to emerge into adults. Don't tie on a dry-fly pattern. Instead, tie on a weighted caddis pupa such as a Gary LaFontaine Olive Deep Sparkle Pupa in size 10 to 14. Use a floating or wet-tip line. Let the fly sink deep. Then lift it up by retrieving and raising your rod at the same time. Let it sink again and repeat the retrieve. Trout will take the fly with a smack. You won't have any trouble telling when you've got one on.

Caddis adults sometimes fly off the surface as soon as they hatch from the pupae. When that is true, it's best to use a pupal pattern, because trout will take few adults. Some caddis adults, called traveling sedges, swim around on top of the surface when they emerge. They swim in circles or straight toward shore. Trout will feed on these, taking them with strong rises. If you see this happening, use any fly that you can skate across the water without sinking. I like to use an Elk Hair Caddis in size 8 to 14. It floats well, has the caddis shape, and won't sink.

I used this method in Chile once, fishing a high Andes mountain lake for landlocked coho salmon. It had been a poor day. My friends and I caught just a few fish. The wind, as always in Chile, made fishing difficult. Then suddenly, just before night, the wind stopped and fish started rising all along the shoreline. I ran down to see what they were taking and saw a size 14 caddis motoring like a boat toward the bank. A small salmon took it with a brutal swirl.

I tied on an Elk Hair Caddis, cast to the same place, and retrieved the fly over the surface as if it were a streamer fished dry. Another fish took it and turned to fight far out into the lake. It weighed only 3 pounds. This lake is so high in the Andes that it is not rich in food, and its fish do not grow terrifically large, even though they are salmon.

I released the first coho, dried the fly, cast to another rise, and had another hit. This fish was bigger. I set the hook too hard and broke it off. It was too dark to tie on another fly. That ended that, but the same thing has happened in many other places.

Midges are sometimes so small that they are as mysterious as lakes themselves seem to be. But they are simple to solve once you realize trout are taking them. Midges live as larvae most of their lives, on and in the bottom silts. Trout take them but not selectively. You don't need to imitate them. Midge pupae rise slowly to the surface. Because they are so small, they often get stuck in the surface film. Trout take them on their way to the top, then again as the naturals are pinned helplessly beneath the surface film. Trout feed selectively and often on the pupal stage of the midge.

Many complicated midge pupa patterns have been invented, but my favorite is still an old one: the Thompson's Delectible Chironomid, or TDC. The original, tied by Washington State biologist Dick Thompson, has a black body, silver rib, and white ostrich herl. I also tie it in tan, red, and green because naturals are common in those colors. It is weighted just a little to get it through the surface film and to start it sinking. I tie it in sizes 14 through 22.

I use adult midge dressings on streams, where they are often important. I do not use them on lakes. Trout take the pupae but do not feed selectively, in my experience, on the adults.

For both damselflies and dragonflies, I imitate only the nymphs and imitate both with the same pattern. That seems a terrible admission, because the nymphs are so different in shape. But here's how I do it. First, I always carry the standard Olive Woolly Bugger in sizes 8 through 12, because it is one of my favorite searching lake flies, and I would never be caught fishing without it. When I find trout feeding selectively to dragonfly nymphs, I pinch off the back half of the marabou tails on a size 8 or 10 Olive Woolly Bugger. The result is a short, fat fly that when wet looks almost like a dragonfly nymph. When I find trout feeding selectively to slender damselfly nymphs, I pinch off the top half of the fibers from the tail of a size 10 or 12 Olive Woolly Bugger, then pinch or cut off all but a few hackle fibers sticking out to each side behind the head, representing legs.

These modified flies both work very well when naturals are out and trout are taking them. You can tie more exact imitations, and they might fish slightly better for you. But I have found that this simplification keeps the fly boxes that I carry all around the world a lot lighter and less confusing.

Scuds are crustaceans, not insects, but trout take them in lakes whenever some insect or other food form is not abundant. Scuds are out there all the time, being eaten by trout. They live in weed beds and swim around like little sticks. Most people see scuds curled up in their hands when they collect them and make the mistake of tying flies for them on curved hooks. The naturals swim straight in the water. Your imitations should be tied on normal hooks with 1X or 2X long shanks. My favorite is the Olive Scud, tied with a shellback of a clear plastic material, such as from a Ziploc bag, in sizes 12 and 14.

Leeches look like fat worms. Some are bloodsuckers, but most that live in lakes eat aquatic insect nymphs and larvae, plus the decaying vegetation and animal matter that collect along the bottom. They undulate along slowly but probably swim fairly fast when they sense that a trout is getting near.

Most leeches that I've collected are either green or black, though a few are dark reddish brown. My favorite patterns for them are Olive, Black, and Brown Woolly Buggers in sizes 6 through 12. I use the Woolly Bugger without modifying it. The pattern fishes for so many different lake food forms that it is the one fly I would not want to be without whenever I'm fishing a stillwater.

It is interesting to note that I've collected leeches up to 4 or 5 inches long, especially in Canadian lakes. But I've never found a trout with a large leech in its stomach. Instead, trout seem always to have one or two leeches in the 1- to 2-inch size range. That is why I use size 8 and 10 Woolly Buggers most often for leeches, though the naturals I collect are often much larger. Trout seem to prefer eating the smaller ones.

Those are not all of the lake flies that I use. This is a short list of flies that fish for the most common kinds of lake food forms. Again, notice that most of the foods are not important in streams or are different from those that trout eat most often in streams.

I find two things very important when you are selecting a lake fly pattern. The first is to always collect from weed beds and along the lakeshore to see what sort of food form is dominant where you are about to cast. Or take a stomach sample if you catch a trout and kill it. Open its stomach immediately and examine what the trout has been eating. That will tell you exactly what to match. It will also build up your knowledge of local lake food forms over a period of years. This kind of knowledge that you acquire will lift you quickly into the category of expert.

The second and most important thing is to carry a separate fly box with flies that match all lake food forms. I have a big box labeled "Lakes" that I carry whenever I'm fishing a stillwater, but never when I'm fishing streams. It contains flies that match lake mayflies, caddisflies, midges, dragonflies, damselflies, scuds, leeches, and a few other foods that are important on my local lakes but might not be important on yours. You'll add your own favorites, but it's very valuable to have a box of flies that is just for lakes.

I desire delicacy for presentation in the rods that I choose for fishing streams. I believe that rods built for distance casting actually hurt your fishing, rather than help it, on moving water. When fishing stillwaters, the opposite is true. The farther you can cast, the less water is disturbed and therefore the more unalarmed trout you can reach, away from your float tube or boat or where you stand wading in the water. Because the area of a circle is mathematically much larger as you increase its diameter slightly, the rod that lets you cast 60 feet rather than 45 feet more than doubles your chances of catching trout.

I recommend a rod 8½ to 9½ feet long, of course in graphite, for a #6 or #7 weight-forward line. It should be a rod that has an action for casting long distances. That means it can be a lot stiffer than the rod that works best for fishing streams.

The reel should hold the fly line plus 100 to 150 yards of backing line. It should also have a high-quality drag system. In lake fishing, you often catch trout much larger than those found in streams. They make long runs. A poor drag will cause you to break them off.

Lines are the most important thing to consider when you select tackle to fish lakes. In streams, nearly all of the fishing is done in water so shallow that the bottom can be reached when you use a floating line. In lakes, you'll often need to fish a lot deeper. In fact, you'll need to be able to fish a variety of depths from 3 feet to as much as 30 feet down. It's critical to choose a line system that lets you fish all of the different depths quickly and with comfort.

You can use one of three kinds of line systems. Any of them will equip you to fish lakes right. The first system combines a floating line with an intermediate, a wet-tip, a wet-belly, and a wet-head line, all in extrafast-sinking. Each of the lines fishes at a different depth. The system lets you fish every depth. The disadvantage is that each line must be carried on a separate reel spool. You must reel in, change spools, and restring your rod each time you want to change lines.

The second system combines a floating line, intermediate, and fast, extrafast, and ultrafast full-sinking lines. Again, each line lets you fish a different depth, and all of the lines together let you explore all the depths of a lake. You must carry each line on a separate reel spool, and you must reel in, change spools, and restring your rod for each change in lines.

The third system, the one I carry for fishing lakes, is a shooting taper system. It combines 30-foot shooting tapers in floating plus slow-, fast-, and ultrafast-sinking. The reel carries 100 feet of shooting line at all times, along with the backing. Each shooting taper has loops at both ends. They can be changed without reeling up and restringing the rod. They are coiled and carried in a line wallet, so there is no need to use a separate reel spool for each line. This is my favorite way to choose lines for lakes. I use the Orvis system of four shooting tapers and have always been happy with it.

In addition to the shooting taper system, I carry floating and wet-tip lines on spools for the same reel. I do this because these are the two lines I use most often. They work perfectly when trout are feeding on the surface or on the bottom of the shallows. Since that is where I find them most often when I fish lakes, I use these two lines most of the time. I use the shooting taper system only when I want to explore the depths, which means that I use it almost always with the fast or ultrafast-sinking heads. If I'm taking a long trip and want to keep my equipment light, I use only the shooting taper system on a single reel spool.

Something to get you afloat and moving on the lake away from the shore can be the most important piece of fishing tackle you can own. If I already owned a stream fishing rod but had no way to get around on a lake, I would buy a float tube before I bought anything else and fish with my old stream rod. The ability to move from place to place is far more important than the ability to cast a long line, because moving is what helps you find the place where trout are concentrated. If you don't fish where they are, it's very difficult to catch them where they're not.

A lake fly box, a lake line system, and a float tube or boat are the only items you need to add to your stream-fishing equipment to fish stillwaters well. The advantage of these three additions is the very small space that they require for storage at home and in the fishing vehicle.

I fish dry flies in lakes only when I see trout rising. The first thing to do is to collect a natural and select a fly pattern to match it. Make sure your leader is 12 to 15 feet long and the tippet long and fine enough for the size of the fly. Dress the fly with floatant, then watch for the next rise within casting range.

Place the first cast to a rise just a foot or two to your side of it. That reduces the chance you will cast the line over the trout and spook it. If the fish does not come to the fly in a minute or so, lift the fly and cast 5 or 10 feet to one side of the rise. That will give you half a chance to catch the trout if it has moved off from the place where it rose. If it does not come to that cast after a half minute or so, lift the fly and cast it the same distance to the other side of the rise, in case the trout has gone that way. In truth, if the trout does not come to the first cast, near the rise, your chances of catching it drop quickly. Wait for another rise and cast to it quickly.

If trout feed in a pod, with several fish cruising and rising together, you must fish dry flies differently than you do to a single rising trout. If you cast to the first rise ring you see, you will probably cast over one or two trout nearer to you and spook them all. It is far better to cast just to the side of the whole pod and hope that one of the trout on the outside edge will see your fly and take it. Or watch the pod carefully and fish only to those that rise on the edge of the pod nearest you. That way, when you hook one, it will not be in the middle of the pod, spooking all of the others.

If a pod of trout is moving, then cast in front and wait for the pod to come to the fly. But again, if you hook the first fish that comes along, you'll spook the rest. If you cast to the front but place the fly where only the trout on your side of the pod can see it, you'll be able to hook a trout and play it to you without disturbing the others.

By fishing a pod of trout carefully, you can sometimes catch four or five fish before spooking all of them. If you do not calculate this out and fish the pod right, you'll catch just one trout and think you've done well.

Trout spend most of their time holding or cruising along the bottom or near submerged weed beds when they are not feeding on the surface. They are almost always taking an occasional mayfly nymph, scud, or damselfly or dragonfly nymph as they swim in and out of the vegetation. Do most of your stillwater fishing with nymphs when trout are not rising to floating naturals or dry flies.

Rig with the line that will get your fly down to the bottom or to the weeds. That usually means a wet-tip line in the shallows, or a fast-sinking line or shooting taper for deeper water. I almost always start with a wet-tip line in lakes if trout are not feeding where I can see them. I fish either along the shoreline or in coves and shallows 3 to 6 feet deep.

Any of the nymphs I've mentioned will work. But think about this: When trout feed on the bottom of the shallows, they most often see natural food forms that are small, olive, and moving slowly because those are the size, color, and behavior of most stillwater trout foods that live in the shallows. Choose a size 12 Olive Hare's Ear or Olive Woolly Bugger, fish it near the bottom or the weeds with a slow retrieve, and your odds of catching trout are excellent. If a specific food form, such as a midge pupa or mayfly nymph, is most abundant in the water you are fishing, be sure to match it in both fly pattern and behavior. Select the right fly, and fish it with the right retrieve. This is my rule for fishing the bottom of the shallows.

One tactic you should never overlook is the combination of a dry fly with a nymph beneath it as a dropper. This works especially well when trout are rising but won't take your dry fly. Examine the natural insect that is hatching. Select a dry fly to match it. Then use your knowledge of lake food forms to select a nymph that looks like the immature stage of the same insect. Chances are that is what those rising trout are truly taking. Tie the nymph to the hook bend of the dry fly on 2 feet of fine tippet. Cast the combination out and let it sit. When your dry fly suddenly is gone off the surface, raise the rod gently to set the hook. You'll have a trout on the nymph.

I use streamers often to fish the shoreline or to explore the depths. The streamer is usually the standard Olive or Black Woolly Bugger. A wet-tip line works best for casting near the shore. Place the streamer a foot or at most 2 feet from the edge. Let it sink briefly. Then bring it toward you with a slow, stripping retrieve. If no trout take it within 10 feet of the shoreline or cover, lift it and cast it to the next bit of shore.

My favorite way to explore a strange lake is to tie a Woolly Bugger streamer to a short leader, say 6 feet, behind the fast-sinking or ultrafast-sinking head of my shooting taper system. Then I cast out behind my float tube or boat and troll slowly around the edge of the lake. I don't go in a straight line parallel to the shore. Instead, I zigzag in and out and fish with fast and slow speeds, so that I might find where the trout are holding at any depth.

Trolling is an excellent way to see some scenery and cover lots of water at the same time. Almost always, you'll bump into a trout somewhere during your tour of the lake. When you do, you'll know that other trout are down there in the same spot. Trout in lakes usually hold or move in schools. If you find one, you've found others. If you haven't found others in that spot, at least you've found the right depth and trolling speed to find more in other places that look just like it. I'll give you an example.

Jim Schollmeyer, the famous fishing photographer, and I were once trolling idly around a lake out in the Oregon desert in early spring. This lake is well known for fat rainbows. But we weren't catching anything that day. We got up on a small hill and looked for rises but saw none. We got into our float tubes and fished the shoreline but caught nothing. After some time, we rigged with streamers for trolling and kicked our way slowly around the lake. We watched birds through binoculars and stayed close enough together that we could talk back and forth, telling lies about all the big fish we'd caught in the past.

We were about 100 feet out from some small, volcanic cliffs rising out of the water just 10 feet or so, when Jim's rod smacked down. He set the hook, yelled, then brought a plump rainbow thrashing to his net. He released it. We then cast out the same amount of line and kept trolling at the same speed alongside the cliffs. My fly got hit next. The trout was a bit bigger than Jim's . . . all of my trout are a little bit bigger than Jim's, of course.

Jim and I trolled down the cliffs another hundred meters but hooked no more trout. So we turned around and trolled right back through the same water where we'd hooked the two fish. Jim's rod jumped again, then a trout jumped far out behind his float tube. A few minutes later, my rod jumped too. That time, I hate to confess, Jim's trout was the biggest one we caught on the trip.

We took a few more trout, then that pod was played out. But we trolled on around the lakeshore. An hour later, we found the same kind of water with little cliffs along the edge and got into some more trout. There was nothing scientific about what we were doing. We were just covering lots of water, showing our flies down in the depths in lots of different kinds of places. Some of those places held trout. When they did, we caught them. That part was not an accident. It has worked so often for us that it's a method we always try when nothing else is working. If you fish lakes enough and learn to do in the future what has worked in the past, it's never an accident when you catch trout. Troll until you find a pod of stillwater trout. Then catch them until they quit.

It's a formula that works almost every time out. It fits right into the larger strategy for fishing stillwaters wherever you go, whenever you fish them: Find the trout, choose the right fly based on what trout eat in lakes, rig the right tackle for the depth you want to fish, then choose the right retrieve for the water, fly, and tackle. When you solve these four simple things, you'll have fish jumping in the air whenever you fish stillwaters for trout.

20

Trout on the Bottom of the Shallows

It's not news that trout hang out in the shallows of stillwaters throughout most of the long fly-fishing season. That's where sunlight strikes to the bottom and prompts vegetative growth. Aquatic insects nibble at the plants. Trout nip at the insects. Trout in lakes and ponds spend most of their time in water just 5 to 10 feet deep because that's where they gather most of their grub.

Most stillwater anglers already know they should sprinkle the majority of their casts over water a few feet deep because they know that's where most trout are caught. Unfortunately most folks expend nearly all of those casts fishing dry flies up top or nymphs, wets, and streamers just a foot or two deep. That's not as wise.

Aquatic insects hide among the plants they browse, or they creep along the bottom itself if that's where they find their food. Instinct tells them that getting caught swimming carelessly far from cover shortens their life expectancies to a swirling abruptness. They don't make that mistake often, and trout know it.

Trout are not entomologists. Like the insects they eat, however, they possess a sure set of instincts for finding food and staying safe. They know that their groceries will nearly always be found hiding in weed beds or hugging the bottom. They also know that a blanket of water pulled overhead is their best protection against predation. As a consequence, except when a hatch tempts them upward or the intense heat of summer drives them out and downward, stillwater trout can be found cruising and feeding in the shallows but near the bottom.

Whenever you arrive at a lake or pond, scan the surface for rise rings that reveal feeding fish. If you fail to find any, immediately suspect that the trout are in shallow water but on the bottom. Adjust your tackle, select your flies, and alter your tactics so that your temptation spends most of its time down where the trout spend most of theirs. Then you'll begin doing more of those dances with trout that are the goal of the game.

The quickest way to adjust your tackle to fish the bottom of shallows just scant feet deep is to continue fishing with your floating line, but add 2 to 4 feet of tippet to your leader and tie on a weighted fly. Cast, then count fifteen to thirty seconds while the fly settles. It will sink 2 to 3 feet, far enough to tempt bottom-bumping trout 3 to 4 feet deep. If you retrieve it slowly, it will remain at that depth. If you use even a moderately fast stripping retrieve with a floating line and weighted fly, the fly will follow the line and ride higher in the water column. That might lift it above the notice of trout.

It's no accident that nearly every experienced stillwater fly fisherman carries a spare reel spool armed with a sinking-tip line. The 10-foot fast-sinking wet-tip is the most versatile of all lines for fishing the bottom of the shallows. Its most effective range is 4 to 6 feet down. If you begin to retrieve right away, with little or no countdown, you can fish a fly just 2 to 3 feet deep. With a count that's a minute or more, the sinking-tip line will deliver your fly as deep as 8 feet. That's about as deep as you can consider to be the shallows.

Once you've found the bottom, whether you use a floating line or a wet-tip, selecting the right fly can require a bit of experimentation. It's impossible to see exactly what trout eat when they've got that blanket pulled over their heads. You can swish a long-handled insect-collecting net through a weed bed or across the bottom, see what's most abundant, and select a fly that looks a lot like it. But that's rarely necessary, because trout are rarely selective when they feed in weed beds and along the bottom. They pluck, instead, at quite a variety of things.

That variety includes swimmer mayfly nymphs, midge and caddis larvae, scuds, waterboatmen, damselfly nymphs, and some large bites like leeches and dragonfly nymphs. It helps to carry dressings roughly resembling each of these groups, but something more simple can be vital to your stillwater success.

You've probably heard the old wives' tale about using a fly the same color as the lake bottom over which you're fishing. It sounds like a myth until you consider that aquatic insects require camouflage to survive. They would never stick around long enough to pass on any DNA if they were not about the same color as the weed beds or the bottom on which they crawl or near which they swim. If you select a generic nymph or small streamer that is the approximate color of the bottom or, even better, any predominant aquatic vegetation, and that looks a little like a lot of the things that trout eat, you won't wait long before cradling a few stillwater trout in your hands.

The bottom is usually some shade of tan or brown. Weed beds are predominantly some aspect of green. Shallow water favorites always include the Gold-Ribbed Hare's Ear nymph and its olive version in sizes 10 through 14. Tan and olive scud dressings in sizes 12 and 14 can almost always be depended upon to coax stillwater trout. Brown and Olive Woolly Buggers in sizes 8 through 12 rarely fail to fool at least a few fish. You'll want to build your fly list beyond those to include imitations of the most common stillwater food forms, filling that separate stillwater fly box I've mentioned. You'll rarely do poorly if you start most of your fishing days with an olive nymph or streamer in size 10 to 14.

Once you adapt your tackle to deliver your fly to the bottom of the shallows and select a fly that looks a little like the creatures that live there, all that remains is to alter your tactics to fool the fish that pal around down there. If you've sampled naturals and selected an imitative pattern, relate your retrieve to the food form your fly imitates. A few types flit about in the weeds or swim boldly but never far from cover. Most of them move very slowy and cautiously when they dare to move at all.

You'll usually do best in stillwaters with a retrieve that is almost painfully patient. Begin by casting and counting the fly down to the bottom. When it begins to fetch weeds on the retrieve, shorten the count a few seconds on subsequent casts. Then hand-twist retrieve the fly back toward you. Roll the wrist of your line hand slowly to retrieve 4 to 6 inches of line with the forefinger. Repeat the roll to gather the same amount of line with the little finger. The slower you hand-twist, the faster you'll catch fish.

Ray Bergman, in *Trout*, cited an incident in which he fished an almost still backwater with a long leader and an early nymph. While his guides watched with disdain, he counted the nymph down to the bottom, then inched it toward the canoe. "My retrieve was about eighteen movements to the minute," he wrote about the speed of his hand-twist, "or about nine complete wrist motions." Almost instantly, he received a vicious strike. "The bored looks on the faces of the guides disappeared," Bergman wrote in his customary quiet and thoughtful voice, "and were replaced by expressions of keen interest."

It's never necessary to count the precise number of hand-twists that you make each minute in order to elicit keen interest from the trout. But it is a way to slow yourself down, and it's safe to say that most of the time when you're fishing nymphs along the bottom of the shallows, it's wise to cut the pace of your retrieve to about half the speed that your natural inclinations goose you into.

Don't stick to the slow hand-twist retrieve when it fails to interest fish after half an hour or so. Some insects, such as mayfly nymphs, swim smartly along, especially when they're getting restless just prior to emergence. A moderately fast stripping retrieve works well when such insects are active, especially if you switch to a wet fly. At times it helps to add a staccato twitching with the rod tip during the retrieve. This makes the fly swim in tiny darts, just like a natural.

At times the bottom and shallow weed beds seem barren of active insects. All are cryptic. None move at any speed. Trout drowse while waiting for something exciting to happen. A streamer fished with a fast stripping retrieve might be just what's needed to startle these lethargic trout into a chase. If the hand-twist with a nymph or slow strip with a wet fly fails to work, try switching to a Woolly Bugger and a retrieve designed to wake up the slumbering trout. The fly should be sunk to a depth that's near the bottom, close along the sides, or over the top of any weed bed you're able to see.

Some weed beds consist of scattered plants that trail up toward the surface, spaced like trees in a thinned forest. Insects live on the stems and leaves. Trout nose among the tall stalks. If you find such a weed bed, you'll be forced to present your fly and make your retrieve right through it. You'll need to get the fly at least halfway to the bottom and use a slow retrieve, because a fast one would agitate the plants every time you hooked up, which you will often. Trout get surprised by such violence and flee. Use the hand-twist and you'll pluck more trout out of these sparse weed beds than you do troubles.

Knowledge of a few narrow options can turn the key to your success when you probe the bottom of stillwater shallows, exploring them for trout. First, use a floating line or wet-tip, and vary the length of your countdown to deliver your enticement to the right depth. Second, experiment with fly patterns based on natural food forms until you find one the trout accept. Third and finally, vary the speed of your retrieve until trout approve by taking consistent whacks at your fly.

You should already be getting a few of those approving takes if you're spending most of your stillwater fishing time casting over water that is at least relatively shallow. You'll begin getting lots more of them when you concentrate your angling effort on the bottom of those same shallows.

21

The Portability
of a Home Lake

I fished an evening with Pete Giampaoli, of Chico, California, on his home lake in the Sierra Mountains. The lake is miles long and excellent for trout, but for some reason it has never been named, or so Pete told me. Creeks, streams, and even a river poke into the large lake along its length, forming delta systems with weedy flats and deep channels that are the old streambeds. As Pete thumped his motorboat toward one of these miniature deltas, he said, "I'd like to be anchored and casting by six-thirty. That's when the trout start moving up."

We arrived at the place at the appointed moment. Pete shut the motor, let the boat coast, and had me slip the anchor just as we passed from deep water over the edge of a shallows. We wound up lined up precisely on the brink of a buried stream channel, about 200 yards out from the actual stream entrance into the lake. Pete had been there the evening before. "Rig with a small weighted nymph about six feet below a strike indicator," he advised me. "Cast upcurrent and let the nymph dangle along the edge of the depths."

I tied a size 14 Olive Beadhead to the tippet, slip-knotted a tuft of yellow yarn to the leader, cast all of 40 feet, then gazed around rather than watching my bobber, which is always my problem. Terns cruised low, their black heads tipped down, peering for fish victims. A flock of white pelicans drowsed on a point across the flats, where weed beds shallowed up so much that trout, Pete told me, dared not cruise until light got low on account of those pouched predators.

Pete hooked the first trout on his small nymph just a few minutes after our arrival. It was a rainbow, about 15 inches long. He released it, cast again, and his indicator dipped down twice more before he got the hook set into another trout. I finally drew my gaze in from the distance and paid attention long enough to notice my own indicator slip under. Moments later, I led the first of a satisfying number of strong rainbows to the boat.

While Pete and I caught fish, a couple other boats motored over, went past us, and anchored in the stream channel. One fellow went way in and plopped his anchor right where the stream became lake. I heard Pete grumble something about this but neglected to jot his precise words in my notebook, so I can't quote him here.

Fishing slowed as darkness drew near. This to Pete was an indication that the trout had moved farther up the channel, toward the shallower water that was now becoming safe territory for them, at least safe from pelicans. But their passage into the stream itself was blocked by that ill-positioned boat.

Pete slipped our anchor and rowed us quietly toward shore. We got out of the boat there and waded into a dilemma. The trout had moved up and were rising all around the boat in which the fisherman, now in near panic at having trout rising just out of range and not being able to catch any, picked up a spin rod and shot out a long cast, reeled something frantically back, dropped the spin rod with a thud, grabbed a fly rod again, and thrashed the water with it. This would have been comical except it was tragic.

Our dilemma was this: It's not polite to move into somebody else's territory, but it's frustrating not to cast onto his water when he's parked where the only trout are rising and light is fading fast. Our choice was to watch him spoil his own fishing and ours or to cast near his boat and risk unsettling his already difficult evening.

I saw a rise 50 feet off his bow. He had his back to it, casting the other way. The trout took my size 18 Parachute Adams. The frustrated gentleman turned to watch me play the fish, and Pete brought up another trout just a short cast aft of the fellow's stern. It was far from our intention to bother him this way, but he'd anchored in the only place where there was hope of action, then banged around, ruining his own chance of having any.

The story goes mildly on, but its meaning has been approached and I'm going to end the action. This was Pete's home lake. Though it was relatively vast, over the years he'd learned that a school of trout would move into that particular stream estuary and begin rising just at darkfall. That's why he motored across the lake to be at that place at six-thirty. What Pete predicted was exactly what happened: Trout moved up and began rising. It might have been the other fellow's home lake, too. But he had not learned it well enough to know that you anchor outside the stream channel, move quietly, and cast to where the trout want to be, not park on their heads and drive them out of casting range.

That evening, Pete and I talked about the kinds of things that you learn by fishing repeatedly on a home lake and the transportability of those bits of knowledge. He said, "What you learn on a home lake will go anywhere in the world and serve you well."

I've got a home lake of my own, of sorts. It's called Lost Lake, likely similar to yours, if you've got one. It's only about 15 acres, nestled in forested hills, surrounded by alders that grow tall alongside it, lean out over it, enrich it by dropping their leaf masses into it each autumn. I grew up fishing it two or three times each summer and continue to fish it at about the same frequency. That doesn't allow the development of day-to-day intimacy, which is what I'd like to have from a home lake. But to get that intimacy, I'd have to give it, and that's not the kind of time I've been able to give this lake.

In return for the minimum time I've invested, I've learned a few things about fishing the lake. One is that fishing is most productive and therefore fun in spring and early summer, when trout are in the shallows feeding on insect migrations and hatches, and it's least productive and fun in late summer, when the water is hot, hatches are slow, and the trout are down. The lake is too shallow to truly stratify, but trout go down 10 to 15 feet and become dour just the same. It's not easy to find and catch them when they do.

These things about seasons are true of almost all lakes: They're excellent in spring and early summer, more difficult in mid and late summer, briefly brisk again in fall. You can take that with you wherever you go. You can also conclude something like this from it: Lakes are best when streams are worst from spring snowmelt and rain, so if you're going to shift your effort from streams to stillwaters, do it then. That is simple enough to sound a little too simple, and in the complexity of different lakes and streams, it might be, but it's also true at most times and in most places and is therefore worth thinking about if you're waiting impatiently for your favorite streams to get into shape, while neglecting nearby lakes that are at that moment at their best.

If I could devote the time to my home lake that I'd like, I could probably figure out just where and how to catch trout consistently when they go down and dour in midsummer. It wouldn't be as much fun as catching them when they're up top and active, though. Somehow, I have the feeling that I'm not missing out on as much excitement as I always think I am. And I know just what I'd be missing if I neglected the Deschutes River then, when caddis hatches are excellent.

These previous notes are related to the annual movements of trout in lakes, from shallow in spring to deep in summer back to shallow again in fall. Time spent on a home lake also teaches you the daily movements within the larger cycle. That's why Pete Giampaoli could go right to that stream entrance at six-thirty in the evening, drop his anchor, and predict the dipping of his indicator. He knew the daily movements of his local trout, into the stream channel at evening, within the larger movement that grouped them just off the channel during the day at the time of year we fished.

On my home lake, I know that trout are going to lift up daily to feed on a midday hatch of *Callibaetis* mayflies beginning in late April and lasting all through May. I also know that as the days get warmer in June, the hatch is going to creep farther toward early morning. In July, I know the hatch will taper off and the trout will rarely show at the surface. I've got to go down and let my fly explore blindly for them or spend the same day meandering over to the Deschutes, where I'll find trout on the banks anxiously awaiting my Deer Hair Caddis. If I decide to go to the river in midsummer, it reflects what I know about my home lake and most others.

This sort of information is portable. *Callibaetis* hatches happen on almost every stillwater, continentwide. It's no secret that you can catch trout on dry flies when trout are on the duns during the hatch and spinners during a flight and fall later in the day. It was revealed only after seasons of sporadic stomach samples on my home lake that trout take about ten nymphs for every adult during a *Callibaetis* hatch, and that an Olive Hare's Ear or Flashback Pheasant Tail will coax trout for hours before and after they will accept a dry.

My home lake has also taught me that any time trout can be seen sipping, but no visible insects are around, some midges must be around; the trout are not likely to be out practicing to improve the delicacy of their riseforms. A pupa pattern dangled a couple feet behind a dry pattern usually solves these midge situations. Often, what is used doesn't matter so much as how it is used: inches deep and drifting idly. Perhaps I shouldn't say that, though. I've solved these mysterious rises to my own satisfaction, often enough, but a lot of casts to sipping rises when midges are on continue to go neglected. Perhaps if I spent more time on my home lake, it would help me understand midge happenings more clearly, and I'd catch more trout. That reflects the basic formula with which I began: The more time spent on a home lake, the more you learn about it, and the more knowledge you've got to take with you to lakes elsewhere.

These are just samples of the lessons you can learn on a home lake and can take with you wherever you fish stillwaters. The key is not any individual bits of knowledge I've mentioned here, but the portability of the body of knowledge to which they add up. You're not likely to learn as much, or learn it nearly so quickly, by fishing a continual scattering of lakes as you are by fishing a home lake repeatedly.

If you spend more time on your favorite lake, it will pay off in trout caught whenever and wherever you fish separate and strange stillwaters.

22

Rod Selection
for Trout Fishing

I've come to an unhappy conclusion: For the average fishing done by the average angler today, it's easier to buy the wrong rod than it is to buy the right one. That's too bad, because the best rods ever made for trout fishing are being made today.

Most of us fish for trout on moving water most of the time. The key to taking trout in that kind of fishing is control over the cast at 25 to 45 feet. The common measure of quality increasingly used by rod makers today seems to be the distance a rod will toss a line. The desire of most fly-shop clerks is to put the rod into your hands that lets them cast farthest. You can't blame them. They're not showing off out there in the parking lot, they're just demonstrating to you that they know what they're talking about. But the distance somebody else can cast with a rod won't help you catch trout if you buy it.

As anglers seek better fishing, they tend to head for more famous waters. There they encounter trout that have been fished over more often than trout elsewhere, trout that are consequently more selective regarding both fly patterns and presentation. So the importance of control over the cast increases as you fish over more sophisticated trout, while the importance of distance decreases.

I'll give you an example. My wife, Masako, and I hiked to the first meadow on Slough Creek, in Yellowstone Park, a couple seasons ago. It was late summer. We expected hopper fishing, but the day was overcast and they were not hopping. It was still a beautiful place to be. We enjoyed that beauty without trout getting involved until a hatch of small olive mayflies started and trout began to rise.

We both did well in the meandering pools that define the Slough Creek meadows. Currents were not complicated there. We were able to coax a few trout with casts that angled up and across the slow flows 30 to 35 feet. We crouched and tilted our rods to the side to keep everything beneath the line of sight of the feeding fish. Our size 18 Olive Harrop Hairwing Duns were sipped often enough to add a new kind of beauty to being in the Slough Creek meadows.

I moved to the head of a pool. A riffle 20 feet wide trotted into the pool at an angle toward the far bank, where it eddied lazily, then headed downstream. The minor riffle delivered a fleet of tiny duns to the eddy. A pod of noses arose to greet them.

It was a slightly difficult situation but not impossible for you or for me. I crouched on the inside of the riffle, cast over it all of 25 feet, and set the fly onto the eddy. Making the cast with a straight line and leader caused instant drag, so I added a couple creative elements to it, which seems to be the average cast over selective trout anymore.

First, I aimed the cast at the eddy, then tipped the rod over to the right to lay the line on the water upstream from the fly. With this reach installed, the riffle whisked the line downstream, introducing slack rather than causing drag. But the leader still straightened in the eddy, and that caused drag.

So second, I added some wiggle to the reach cast. That's not difficult: just wobble the rod tip as the line lays over. The line lands in S-curves. Wobble early and the curves land in the leader. Wobble late and the curves land back near the rod. I wiggled my rod as soon as I started to lay it over for the reach, and the leader landed with lots of slack in it. This let the fly sit idly in that eddy for thirty seconds or so before the fly began to drag. By then, most often, one of those noses poked out to take it. I'd lift the rod slowly to take out the slack and slip in the hook. Do it fast and you rip the fly out of there on a miss, which can ruin the rest of your fishing.

After surprising a few trout, I called Masako up to join me. I explained the problem with the currents, told her how to solve it. She's a fine caster. I knew she could do it. But to my surprise, her line and leader landed straight time after time, and the fly left a wake in its hurry to get out of that eddy. It was frustrating for her. Because I had relinquished the fishing, it was just as frustrating for me. I tapped my foot.

Masako held out her rod and said, "Show me."

It would be easy. I made an abrupt backcast and forward cast and leaned into the reach. As the line unfurled, I wobbled the rod back and forth. Nothing happened. The rod was too stiff to respond. I repeated the cast, trying harder to insert those S-curves into the line. When the rod finally consented to wobble, it waved widely over its entire length, rather than narrowly out at its end. The curves that fell to the water were too broad to do any good, and the cast was so difficult to control that I missed the eddy anyway.

Silently, I indicated to Masako that she should try the cast with my rod. She lofted the line, leaned over, and wiggled the rod. The fly landed in the eddy and sat awhile. A trout tipped up to take it.

Masako writes for Japanese fly-fishing magazines. Her rod was very expensive. She was astonished to learn that it simply would not execute the cast needed to bring those particular trout to her fly. I spent the rest of the day carrying that costly stick while she delighted in making curve casts and wiggle casts and reach casts with the rod I'd chosen for what I call my presentation rod because it did precisely those things so well.

What sort of rod gives the control that is so beneficial for trout fishing on moving water? Not the kind designed solely to fling your fly over the horizon. Those are excellent for steelhead and salmon, for bonefish and barracuda, even for trout fishing on lakes. They're in demand for good reason. For the fishing most of us do most of the time, however, they're the right rod in the wrong place.

The sort of rod that works best for trout fishing on moving water has a different description. I hate to define its action in the traditional terms of fast, medium, or slow because that says so little about the way a rod is put together and what it will do. A better set of terms has been around for a while. Skip Morris's *The Custom Graphite Fly Rod* is a very fine book that has been read by far too few folks. In it, he described rod actions in terms of stiff-butted, medium-butted, and soft-butted. These terms tell you a bit about how a rod is built, and therefore a lot about how it will act when you cast it.

A stiff-butted rod has the same unrelenting firmness from butt to tip. This causes it to form the tightest of line loops. When loaded, the rod cocks like a spring. When released, the spring tosses that tight loop a long way. This design is excellent for distance casting.

A medium-butted rod has more flex toward its tip than in the lower length. If you cast short, the tip will carry the line. You can load most such rods down into the butt and cast for distance. If you wobble a medium-butted rod while the line is in the air, the more flexible front end will respond while the butt does not. If you wobble it narrow, almost a quiver with your wrist, you get tiny S-curves. If you wobble it wide, the line lands in big S-curves. You've got the idea now: If you do something different to the rod, the rod does something different to the line. That is called control.

A soft-butted rod has the same relative softness from end to end. You're back to where you were with a stiff rod, only now you have open loops rather than closed. When you wave the rod for the wiggle cast, it ambles back and forth over its entire length. Your S-curves on the water look like the laziest of snakes out for a swim. You'll have little more control over the placement of those loops than you would if they were that snake. It's nearly impossible to get slack out to the line tip and leader, where you usually want it most.

How do you tell if a rod is right for trout before you buy it? You can flex a rod in your hand and tell a little about where it has its stiffness, and therefore a little about its action and how it will cast. But you won't be able to tell much about a rod unless you cast it. When you do, remember those distances at which you'll be fishing it: 25 to 45 feet. If you can't cast short with a rod, it's not a good one, even if it will stack an impressive pile of line against the fence at the far end of the fly-shop parking lot.

Most medium-butted rods will toss the line 60 to 80 feet if you need that to happen. It's fun to see if a rod will cast that far when you test-drive it. You should be more concerned, though, that the rod lets you open and close the line loop at more restricted ranges. It's also more important that the rod responds when you wobble it and puts the curves in the line where you want them to land on the water.

Whenever you try out a new rod, keep that word *control* in mind. That's what will help you catch trout. That's what you should try for in the fly-shop parking lot. Cast at fallen leaves and paper cups and paint spots on the pavement and buttercups in the grass. Make sure you can hit them, or place a fly very near them, at trout-fishing ranges. Cast for delicacy: See how softly you can coax the line to land on what will later be water if you decide to buy the rod. If it lands with a smack no matter what you do, ask to cast another, unless your goal is to frighten some fish.

I had the good fortune to prowl the aisles at the most recent Fly Tackle Dealer Show. In the waning hours, I visited several booths and asked to try what the makers considered their best presentation rods. That's when I discovered the vast number of rods that grandly surpass anything that was available, at least to me, when I started in this sport.

The best rods ever made, for the fishing that most of us do most often, are being made today. Each of those makers offered at least one very fine fly rod for fishing trout on moving water. Some had several that were excellent. The problem is to pick out the rod that works best for what you want to do from the full rack of rods that work as well or better, but for what somebody else wants to do.

23

Traveling Trout Flies

I got a letter not long ago from a gentleman preparing to visit Oregon for the first time, asking me what flies he should tie or buy for a trip to the Deschutes. That's my home river. I began a long answer, listing most of the standards, when I suddenly broke off. I realized that I no longer think in terms of specific flies to take to certain rivers, even the one I fish most often. Instead, I wrote him, I always carry a couple fly boxes, one for dry flies and one for sunk, that I attempt to keep stocked with a set of dressings that will fool trout wherever I might go. I carry other fly boxes, of course, and add other dressings. But most of my fishing is done out of those two basic boxes, on the Deschutes and everywhere else.

The results of this thinking cut in several directions. The most obvious is having flies that work wherever I wind up, which these days is just as often at some far-flung destination as it is my home Deschutes. Another result is a reduction in my burden, therefore freedom in my fishing if I'm traveling any distance on foot.

The largest result of concentrating on carrying flies that work everywhere is simplicity in my fly tying. You know how it goes when you tie two of this and two of that: It's an easy way to tangle up your fly boxes. I don't disdain that type of tying; I do it all the time, especially when trying to work out the best dressings for a certain hatch. If you're going to tie in dribbles, then buy a few small fly boxes. Use one for each hatch you fish often. Keep these experimental ties separate from your main body of flies.

John Gierach wrote somewhere in that bright string of books of his that you tie flies by the dozen, not by the ones and twos. That's important thinking. If a fly is worth trying, it's worth tying enough to give it a fair trial. If a fly is worth carrying in a basic set of dependable dressings, then you'd better have at least a dozen at the start of a long trip or you're bound to be in trouble by the end of it. One pattern is going to work better than all others, probably for a reason as simple as that it works on the first day of the trip so you keep using it. On the third day, you'll run low even if you tie by the dozen as John suggests.

The tying simplicity gained by the two basic fly boxes is this: They give me clear direction about which flies I need to tie by the dozen. If my size 8 Olive Woolly Buggers are running low, which they just did on a trip to Chile, then it's time to sit down and tie a dozen to refill that empty row in the ripple foam fly box. If my size 16 Parachute Adamses dwindle toward the bottom of the box, which they do on almost every trip, then I know it's time to sit at the vise and fill that compartment back to spilling over.

Tying right into the boxes between trips adds an elemental pleasantness, because each fly tied is dropped into the slot from which the fly it's replacing was removed. As you tie, you recall the moment in which the previous Olive Woolly Bugger got whacked away by a brutal brown trout in Chile, or when the earlier Parachute Adams got snicked off when a sipping rainbow on the Bighorn or Bow had more heft than you anticipated when you set the hook.

If you accept this concept, the flies you tie for your own basic boxes should arise out of your own success, not mine. Most of that success and selection of flies will happen on your own home waters. But be assured that what happens at home will travel well. If the Royal Wulff becomes your favorite searching dry fly, tie it in a range of sizes and you'll catch trout on it in a surprising range of situations. Your own experience will lead you to that conclusion, after you've fished the fly long enough. But history will also tell you the same thing and help you choose your set of flies. One reason to try a fly in the first place is many long seasons of success behind it in the hands of lots of other tiers and fishermen. Flies don't get famous if they fail to catch fish.

Donny Williams, the noted Livingston, Montana, guide, tells a story about driving British hosts nuts by fishing size 20 Royal Wulffs over their selective chalkstream trout and taking lots of them. I'm not recommending that you use your traveling fly boxes to goad folks with noses tipped up like goats. But it will happen, and you'd be wasteful not to enjoy it.

I am recommending that you tie whatever flies you choose in a range of sizes, so that they will work in a range of situations. It's well known that trout are interested in three aspects of any fly pattern: its size, form, and color, in that order of importance. Often, if you get the size right, you have no other problems to solve except getting the fly in front of the trout in a manner that makes it look alive.

Your two traveling fly boxes will be far more versatile if they cover the most common shapes, sizes, and colors of the natural food forms on which trout feed most often. My own favorites include Harrop Hairwing Duns for mayflies, tied in olive, sulfur, brown, and gray, each color in sizes 12 through 16 and some through size 20. You'd be crazy not to carry something like the Elk Hair Caddis in tan, gray, and brown, sizes 10 through 16. Midges are mandatory in gray, tan, and olive, sizes 16 through 22. But these are just the basic drys and should be augmented with searching flies such as the Royal Wulff and Humpy in sizes 10 through 16. You need a few flies to cover beetles and ants and hoppers.

Sunk flies should cover a short list of nymphs, wets, and streamers. I carry the Gold-Ribbed Hare's Ear, Whitlock Fox Squirrel, Herl Nymph, and Muskrat in sizes 10 through 16, all slightly weighted. The outcome is obvious: With these four dressings, I've covered the four basic colors in which natural nymphs and larvae arrive. I add Charlie Brooks's Montana and

Brown Stones, stout and tied in the round, because I use them during salmonfly and golden stone migrations, but also because their use has extended successfully into many searching situations. I expect to catch trout when I fish them. That is most of what any short list of flies is all about, for any type of fish: faith in each dressing, based on past connections to whatever you're after.

The confidence factor is why I would never be without a supply of a certain beadhead nymph that, as far as I know, doesn't even own a name. I first tied a dozen of them on a picnic table beneath the spreading leaves of a shade tree in the backyard of Andy and Marie Davidson's home in the rolling limestone hills near Mount Horeb, Wisconsin. The whimsical size 12 tie has a brass beadhead, olive dubbed body, and yellow thread rib. That's it.

It took an enjoyable hour to tie the dozen on the Davidsons' picnic table, listening to the birds sing. Later in the week, I met Ted Leeson, author of *Habit of Rivers,* and we fished the spring streams rising from those limestone hills. It took just two days to lose those dozen beadhead nymphs to fat trout. The pattern was so successful for me that I had to settle onto another picnic bench in a streamside campground during fishing time and replenish them in my box of sunk flies. The dressing has a permanent place there now, though it still does not have a name. But it's likely that any other beadhead nymph would have worked as well.

Muddlers plus Woolly Buggers in black and olive, all in sizes 6 to 12, cover a wide range of streamer situations. I carry a few of the speckled wets popularized by Sylvester Nemes in *The Soft-Hackled Fly:* Partridge and Orange, Partridge and Yellow, Partridge and Green. I add traditional Blue-Winged Olive, Black Gnat, and Alder wets to cover other parts of the color spectrum, all in sizes 10 through 14.

I also carry odds and ends like my favorite Beetle Bug searching dry, the Griffith's Gnat for crippled midges, the Parachute Adams because it's excellent at mismatching hatches and still fooling lots of trout. The assignment here is to devise your own list of favorites and to outfit your own boxes of dry and sunk flies that take trout wherever you might hike. Don't just copy my list.

I originally began tying into and fishing out of two fly boxes in order to make my burden lighter on long days astream and to decrease my tying time. Lately I've discovered an added advantage. By selecting a list of flies that covers the spectrum of natural trout foods, I've found that I carry a killing fly more often, rather than less often, than I did when I carried lots more fly boxes but a less careful selection of flies. Sometimes—not always—I actually catch more trout on account of carrying fewer flies.

24

Minimum Kit

I was encouraged to pare my gear early in my fly-fishing career due to the difficulties of the tiny mountain streams that I still call my secret home waters. These streams have dangers. They tumble down the hills in long successions of waterfalls and cascades broken by occasional plunge pools. The rushing water pauses long enough in these pools to offer slight comfort to small pods of cutthroat trout before bounding on toward the next brink.

Some of these tiny streams are fished along less than they are ascended. Rick Hafele, coauthor of *Aquatic Insects and Their Imitations,* and I still take a minor annual trip to the Oregon coast stream where Rick did his master's studies on aquatic insects. We take one fly rod and one camera and leapfrog the pools, taking turns casting and capturing the action on film. Many of the resulting photos show one or the other of us clinging to keep balanced on a car-size boulder with one hand and hoisting a trout flapping into the air with the other.

When rock-hopping and climbing such difficult terrain, it adds danger if you have a full creel dangling off your shoulder, as we did in the old days, or a loaded vest draped around your neck, as we do more commonly in the present. Creels and loaded vests swing when you leap. The momentum of either can topple you off a fragile balance when you land. If your conveyance carries any excessive amount of weight, that sows the seeds for disaster. I harvested enough of those, early on, to begin carrying precisely what I needed and never any extra.

For those tiny streams, fished in my early days with dry flies and no others, my minimum of gear became a single Sucrets tin filled with drys, a bottle of fly floatant, two spare tippet spools in 4X and 5X, plus a pair of fingernail clippers to trim leader knots. It all fit easily in a couple shirt pockets. It all worked fine on my home waters. When I fished them, I knew that was all I'd ever need.

I made the mistake of carrying this same minimum amount of gear on a couple trips away from my small streams. I caught trout as long as they were willing to take dry flies and, further, were willing to take one of the few attractor patterns that I carried. But this minimal set of flies and other items failed me miserably whenever trout fed selectively on the surface, fed a few inches to a couple feet deep, or stayed on or near the bottom and fed strictly on nymphs, which, as we all know, they are instructed by their mentors to do exactly 80 percent of the time.

So the problem, when I desired a minimum of gear but also to travel, became the addition of versatility to simplicity. This problem arrived at about the same time the creel got reinvented in the form of the miniature belt bag. I bought an original Side-kick II from Wood River Company and have never seen any need to expand from there, though many similar products are now on the market to solve the same problem. Some are belt bags; others are chest bags; many are condensed vests. I can only advise you to look them all over, decide which size and kind you'd like to carry, then dedicate yourself to never exceeding its comfortable capacity. There's little use selecting something small, then stuffing it with all you used to carry in something large.

Think in terms of backpacking—where a minimum of gear is not only most desirable, but is also most clearly defined. You don't want to carry any extra weight; you also don't want to get caught without something you might need to solve the most common set of angling situations. Unless you're hopelessly into catch and release, your dinner might depend on your ability to con a trout from a forested stream or an alpine lake that holds them in overabundance.

The main way the miniature kit, as opposed to nothing but your shirt pockets, allows versatility is its capacity to carry a couple fly boxes of some size. They need not be large ones but should be big enough to hold a range of both searching and imitative dry flies, plus a fair selection of nymphs, wets, and streamers. These, along with the few trinkets needed to fish the different sorts of flies successfully—listed at the end of this chapter—allow the solution of situations at the three levels you'll always encounter: the surface, mid-depths, and bottom. Most of the flies in my own two boxes are standards, but of course I include many of my favorites, as you should yours.

A light minimum kit eliminates the swing and tug of a load of gear. It can be cinched around your waist or snugged tight to your chest. When you leap, it does not build any momentum going in the opposite direction from you. When you climb, you can shift a belt bag around to the small of your back or tuck a chest pack under an arm, and you'll have nothing between you and the boulder you need to belly against. Paring your gear to a minimum, and carrying it strapped tightly to you, adds an element of safety if you fish my favorite kind of water. But that is far from the only reason to reduce your equipment and carry it in a minimum kit. Comfortable travel is another.

One of my favorite complexities of streams is in the headwaters of the Cisnes River system in southern Chile, at Estancia de los Rios. Hafele and I are packing for a trip there now. We'll be fishing big water that's easy to navigate, small streams that are choked by brush, spring creeks that frighten you with the size of the trout that cruise them and pick selectively at next-to-nothings. We need to go prepared for all of those situations, but we also need to backpack to reach some of the best of them. I'd like to carry a vest stuffed with the solutions to all possible problems, but it would make my pack far too heavy, and Rick hasn't agreed to carry it for me. I'll take my vest, in case Rick relents, but I'll be packing my minimum kit for the more likely outcome.

I had the little kit along last year on an exploratory trip to the same system of rivers. I also had my standard vest. While the trip remained standard—driving out in rigs to fish a few hours, driving back to the lodge for lunch or dinner—I tucked a full array of gear in the vest and carried it without complaint. Then the fishing farther out from the lodge got more intriguing to me—it was exploring—and I found myself galloping long distances across rolling pampas every day to get onto new water. The vest became too much of a burden. The belt bag came out, made both hiking and fishing a lot more fun, and allowed me to cover some water and catch some trout that I would not have had enough ambition to reach had I been more heavily laden.

I'm no advocate of throwing away the fly-fishing vest. In most stream and river situations, it's the best way to carry your gear. But I advise that you track down and outfit some sort of minimum kit that suits the variety of places you pursue trout and the special ways in which you enjoy placing yourself in that pursuit. Don't assemble a kit that outfits you for what I like to do, which, when I'm carrying my minimum kit, is mostly pestering trout in tiny streams, unless that's what you like to do, too.

Put some time and thought into tailoring a minimum kit for the kind of trout fishing you like to do most. Keep it light and strapped on tight. It will deliver you to places, and to fish, that you might otherwise never encounter.

Author's Minimum Kit:
Sidekick II belt bag
leader clippers
combined scissors/pliers/hemostat tool
dry-fly floatant and line-cleaning pad
spare leaders in 7½ and 10 feet
tippet spools in 3X, 4X, 5X, and 6X
nontoxic split shot and yarn strike indicators
handkerchief to dry and clean flies
two fly boxes: one for drys, one for sunk flies

25

Old Good Stuff

I sat in sunshine on a bench of grass that was cropped short by flocks of wild Andean geese, alongside the River of Swans in southern Chile. I patiently dressed my fly line in preparation for a day tossing hopper drys to bank-feeding browns. The young and soon to be famous Chilean guide Sebastian Letelier fidgeted next to me, watching the water for the occasional nose that poked out, wishing I'd get fishing.

I was in no hurry. Fishing had already been excellent in all of the previous days I'd been on the river. It was pleasant in that warm and windless moment to sit and slip the old green fly line through the saturated felt pad of line dressing. That pad was once white; now it's nearly black from so many years of fly lines run through it alongside so many rivers.

When I finished dressing the line, I returned the pad to the dented and worn yellow tin that came with the fly line when I bought it. That statement alone gives you a hint about the age of the line if you've been fishing for a while. Today that same line is sold with just the pad in a Ziploc bag, though the pad still performs its job perfectly and will, if you buy one now, someday become old and black and just as good as mine.

While stretching the line out onto the grass, I came to the inch-long black splice where the line got caught on something about five years ago and somehow managed to get itself cut clean through. I was on a horse trip far into the headwaters of the Yellowstone River at the time, outfitted by Merritt and Barbara Pride out of Lost Fork Ranch in Cameron, Montana. I had a tiny fly-tying kit with me. So I sat on a different bench of grass alongside a different river and twirled the bobbin and black thread around the stripped and overlapped ends of the fly line, until the splice was an inch long and as strong as the line itself.

I'd intended to replace the line as soon as I returned from the wilderness. But the splice accidentally marks about the right place to hold this weight-forward line when a long cast is to be shot, and it causes no more than a slight aesthetic disturbance as it emerges into sight off the reel. So I decided not to replace the line back then and continue to use it now, especially on adventures far from home where I want to use things that I know work.

The great young Sebastian saw the splice run through the felt pad. He said, "What's that?" He assumed it was a clever mark I'd made in the line by intention. I should have lied and told him he was right, but instead I told him the truth and I think lowered myself slightly in his esteem. That's all right; a lot of my old gear has that same effect on those who follow the latest in fly-fishing gadgetry.

There is a reason, far beyond nostalgia, that I continue to use that spliced fly line. The line is the precise right balance for the rod on which I use it. That rod was a gift Skip Morris gave me after I wrote the foreword for his book *The Custom Graphite Fly Rod*. The rod, as you can easily guess, has a special place in my long list of gear. But it holds that place not just because it's a gift from Skip. It's also the perfect rod with which to explore the river or lake in the next county or on the next continent. I don't use the rod and the spliced line often, because I want the rod to last forever. But it's the outfit I take when a trip is important and I want to know my gear will work, which is why I was using it on that horse trip in Yellowstone and that distant trip to the River of Swans in Chile.

The rod is a four-piece, 8½ feet long, rated for a double-taper 5-weight line. With the weight-forward 6-weight, it feels light and crisp, casts long or short, gives me an excess of that thing you know I desire and also demand from any fly rod: control of the cast at any distance. The line is wound on an old Scientific Anglers System One reel.

Rick Hafele and I still use the SA reels given to us when we worked together on his *Anatomy of a Trout Stream* video more than a decade ago now. Rick picked up my outfit briefly on that same trip to Chile and spooled off line to make a cast. The reel squawked at him. He said, "What the hell have you done to this thing, Dave?"

I reached over, removed the spool, fingered some Vaseline onto the neglected reel post, and replaced the spool. It instantly calmed the squawking, returning the reel to its quiet, dependable self. The reel was built to survive, and it has. It's had to. I won't bore you with a list of its accidents, but it's still reeling line right, is still dependable, and still has a sound that I like when a trout smacks my fly and makes a dash for the far bank.

That reel carries the memories of when Rick and I worked on that video together. It also carries the spliced line and 100 yards of backing. It attaches nicely and looks good—at least to me, and I'm the one who counts in this matter—on the fly rod that Skip Morris built for me. With a spare spool armed with a wet-tip line, I feel I'm fairly well prepared for nearly anything I might encounter in the kind of fly fishing I prefer to do most, which is roughly exploring for trout.

The outfit is excellent for exploration. When you're exploring, the least desirable thing is some surprise in your equipment. That's why old good stuff is often the best to be carrying when you're far from home, though it's often not quite as pretty or, to be honest, always as perfect in performance as new good stuff. By the time it gets to be old good stuff, though, you know precisely what it will do and what you can do with it in any situation.

I could go on to tell you about my fly vest. I've replaced it twice now with new ones but bounced back to using the old one both times because I got tired of frisking myself every time I wanted to find something in one of the new vests. The old vest is no longer made. It's not as good as a lot of new ones I know about. But when I'm wearing the one that's been surrounding me for about fifteen years now, I know everything's address.

My tippet spools are on the right side in one tiny outside pocket, my split shot and strike indicator yarn in the one next to it. That dented yellow tin of line dressing hides behind the tattered half of a handkerchief I use to wick moisture off my dry flies after catching a trout, before I dress them with the North Fork squeeze bottle of floatant that's been dangling from the same D-ring for about ten years now. When the old floatant tube nears empty, I refill it and throw the new bottle away. They don't make the one that dangles anymore, at least not in blue.

If stuff is old and you selected it carefully for durability in the first place and you've used it for a long time, then it's not nearly as likely to let you down as something you've used only briefly, say four or five years. In addition to durability, there's the benefit of familiarity. Old good stuff is simply equipment that extends itself from you. You don't have to ask it any questions.

It's not likely that you're going to keep and constantly use something that doesn't suit you and who you are and what you do. If you're the kind of person who sits in the grass in the sunshine and patiently dresses a line with a five-year-old splice in it, the new quick rods with actions like axe handles are probably going to piss you off. You'll try them. You'll probably even buy one or two, because they're such magnificent casting tools. But they're not likely to get included on your list of gear that goes with you on trips.

On the opposite hand, if you live in a slightly swifter world, then you'll be more satisfied with a faster rod and newer line and a reel with a finish that hasn't been worn down and dented. I recommend it. Just be sure to use the same setup long enough and often enough that it grows into old good stuff. That way you know what it will do and what you can do with it in any situation. Just as important, you know what it won't do and what you can't do with it.

You have to be curious and try new gear. Trying new stuff is the only way to discover what deserves to become old stuff.

Once you've found what's right for you, then use it consistently enough that you will know what the group of you—you and your outfit and your vest or minimum kit and your peripheral gear and even the wader bags and rod cases that convey it all—can accomplish together.

26

Getting It Together

Masako and I just returned from what amounted to a first spring trip, though it happened in late fall. We went to a favorite small river not far from home for just a couple days. Trout rose to hatches of invisibles both days, as they nearly always do on this river. The trout were not large, but their size was magnified by their willingness to sip an emerger or dry fly if it was close to what was hatching and the presentation was almost flawless.

The sun was out and faintly warm, just as it is when the river, its insects, and its trout begin to awaken at the early end of the year. A few robins sang in the sage alongside the river, though their songs were just murmurings compared with all the shouting they'd done in spring.

The real reasons this late trip was like a spring tune-up to us were the baby who kept us bouncing after her all spring and summer, then surgery on my casting shoulder that knocked me out for most of the fall. We hadn't been able to get out much all year. When we went to this river, saw the trout rising, and heard the robins singing softly, it was more like a first spring trip than a fall reprise following a normal summer spent fishing. We'd never had time to tune our gear.

My main regret was getting out to the river before, rather than after, the bit of tweaking it takes to be ready to solve the situations that fly fishing presents. My advice is to get out your vest and all your other gear, no matter what time of year it might be, spread it out on the floor, and frisk it for problems.

If you haven't filled your fly boxes yet, then jot a list of what you need, tie or buy them by the dozen or half dozen, and drop them right into the empty compartments that beg for them. If you're like me, you'll begin your season with many flies missing. They'll always be the most important ones, because those are the ones you use, and therefore lose, most often.

Second to flies, what gets used most and therefore will most often cause you preparation problems are leaders. I no longer tie my own. Instead, I buy knotless base leaders in 7½- and 10-foot lengths, tapered to 3X. I can fish them as they are with streamers or big nymphs, add a tippet of 4X or 5X to fish average trout flies, or tie in transition sections and add a tippet of 6X or even 7X to fish tiny flies. To accomplish this, I carry spare tippet spools in 3X, 4X, 5X, 6X, and 7X, all from the same manufacturer as the leaders so knots are strong.

When we arrived at the river that late-fall day, the first thing I did was get out my 5X tippet and tug the last foot of leader off the spool. I wanted 3 feet of it, but the spool was empty. I used that last foot for a transition to 6X, which worked fine where we were. Had we been on the Deschutes River, I'd have been in more trouble than the trout.

The next problem I ran into was a 4X spool that must have been a couple years old. It popped before the 6X, which meant losing a tippet every time I lost a fly. Modern leader material weakens fairly quickly. Some smart folks I know write the date on a tippet spool when they buy it, and then throw it away after a year. I'd recommend that, or just getting fresh spools each spring, and always before a major trip. Then keep an eye out to make sure there's still some leader left on every spool, especially the ones you use the most. For me, that's 5X, which is why it's the one I always empty to my own surprise in the middle of a trip if I'm not watchful.

If you fish nymphs much, you'll have the same problem Masako ran into that day. She carries a dispenser with several sizes of nontoxic split shot but most often uses just one size. During a dull moment between hatches, she decided to launch a nymph rigged with indicator and shot. But she found that the one size she wanted was gone, while all the others she did not want were present. You can buy nontoxic shot refills, but they're difficult to find when you've already got your feet in trout water. Keep a refill around, replenish your supply between trips, and you won't run into that problem.

I could get into a litany of the other problems Masako and I encountered due to our lack of preparation. I had to quit fishing when the sun broke out bright and fetch my sunglasses from the rig because they weren't tucked in the vest pocket where they belong. Masako couldn't find the bandanna with which she dries her fly after it's taken a trout. My squeeze tube of floatant was empty. She had no wading chains to slip over her felts, and the rocks on that river were invitations to disaster. I had no lip balm with sunscreen in it. She had no itch medicine to calm the bite of an angry ant. I collected an interesting mayfly, went to pickle it in alcohol, and found that the two vials I always carry were already crammed with an unsortable tangle of insects from everywhere. I'd failed to key them out, label them, and replace the vials after the last trip.

Most of the problems we had were the result of things we'd failed to do after the last trip. The best time to get ready for any next trip is always when you put things away from the last one. When you're out fishing, you notice what you need to replace. If you're smart, you'll replace it as soon as you get home. If you're like me, you make a mental or even penciled note about it, then get home, toss the gear into storage, and forget all the things you meant to do until you're out on the water again the next time and it's too late to do them.

While you have all of your trinkets out of the vest, scattered for inventory and repair, give the vest itself some thought. Decide the best location for each item you carry in it. When you put things away, put them where they are handy in relationship to the number of times you use them each day. You don't want to dig for flies, floatant, or tippet spools. It's not a problem if you have to stop and unzip a pocket to get out your wading chains, because you'll have to wade to shore to put them on anyway.

When you put each item away in your vest, be sure it's ready for the next trip: fly boxes full, tippet spools with leader on them that's fresh and strong, floatant dispenser full, handkerchief handy, hemostats and sunglasses and sunscreen and everything else you use present and accounted for and where you know you can find them. When you're fishing and use something, put it back where you got it, and you'll soon be able to locate any item without a search warrant. If you need to pat yourself down every time you want anything from your vest, you're assigning yourself a lot of needless frustration.

When you've finished with your vest, you're just getting started. Examine your rods, reels, and lines. Wax ferrules, grease spindles, replace lines that are all cracked up. If your waders have holes in them, just after a trip is never a bad time to locate and fix them.

I'll mention just one final problem before I depart to inventory my own gear. I keep a wader bag, a big old thing so heavy it's probably what caused me to need the shoulder surgery, packed with everything I expect to need on a fishing trip. I can grab this bag and head out the door and know I'm not forgetting anything . . . if I've taken time to put everything in it after the last trip.

After the last trip before the tune-up I took with Masako, I'd removed the thick cotton sweatpants I usually wear under my waders, no doubt to wash them. I did not put them back. The water was nippy on the river we fished that late-fall day. I didn't have anything except thin pants to wear under my waders. That lack of preparation after one trip caused me to have to do some dancing on the next.

27

Remaining Ready

For a long time in my fly-fishing life I suffered a pair of problems, both arising from the same evil root: too much stuff. The first problem was the agonizing amount of time spent getting ready for any fishing trip, no matter how brief, and then the same amount of time spent untangling myself from everything after the trip was over. Whether I went for a day to my home Deschutes, a week to the meccas in Montana, or a month to distant Chile, it was all relative: I spent as much time getting ready and then unready as I spent being wherever I was going.

The second problem was the excess energy I squandered while on trips dealing with gear that I carried but rarely used. My stabs at fishing should have been clean but were not because of all the gear I owned and felt required to carry along. Part of the price of any item, whether a rod, reel, float tube, or drift boat, is the necessity that you find a way to use it in order to justify owning it.

A third problem arose out of the first two. I began to arrive consistently at wherever I was going to discover that I'd forgotten one or two things that I truly needed. I usually assumed they were stashed somewhere among the two or three bushels of stuff that it turned out I did not need and wished I'd left home. Once the item I discovered missing, at the launch ramp on a day float, turned out to be my reel. I was forced to sit and gaze at rising trout all day while gliding down one of the world's finest trout streams. My rig had already been shuttled, so I felt compelled to launch.

That day propelled me toward solving the riot among my equipment. I arrived at a solution that killed most of the problems with the same thrown stone and further satisfied me by not decreasing my fly-fishing possessions but actually slightly increasing them.

I did not pare my gear to a minimum but instead winnowed out of it a minimum of essential gear and set it aside in a separate pile, got it organized and packaged, filled it out with this trinket and that so nothing was missing for a trip of any duration, then kept it constantly prepared for any trip I might like to take without the normal logistical nightmare of packing. This was clever because it left me with all my old complication of stuff for those times when I'd still like to take a really tangled trip.

This condensation of gear now resides in an oversize and excessively pocketed blue daypack, designed just for fly fishing. It could as well be a shoulder bag, boat bag, wader bag, grocery bag, or any other kind of container that could be slung over a shoulder or hoisted onto a back. It's not required to be blue. Leaning against the closet wall alongside the daypack is a green double-barreled rod carrier that holds a light presentation rod and a medium nymphing rod with their reels always attached. I'm after trout. If you take different kinds of trips than I do, you should arm yourself with different kinds of gear.

By keeping the daypack and rod tube packed and ready, I'm always prepared to grab them and go fishing without fear that I'll arrive lacking something I need when I put on the brakes at stream, pond, or lakeside. A key to this is completing the collection. Don't leave tippet spools, hemostat, and sunglasses in your overstuffed vest that is not a part of this kit, or in your major pile of tackle that is left when you've completed it, thinking you'll not forget to transfer them when it's time to pack up your minimum gear and go. Outfit the daypack completely and separately, not dependent on anything to be extracted from the larger set of gear you might use most often, though if you're like me, once you get this daypack fitted out, your main mound of gear might become more and more neglected.

My favorite fly shop had a fairly brisk day when I decided to pare my gear to a minimum. I had to go out and buy duplicates of quite a few things I already owned, in order that my daypack might be constantly ready to serve. That's why I enjoyed a slight increase, not decrease, in the number of angling possessions. Be warned about that.

Essential to this system is some sort of chest pack, belt pack, or shorty vest that fits inside the daypack. I use a Wood River Sidekick II belt bag. It looks suspiciously like the canvas creel my dad still carries and that is, of course, an anachronism; his has a compartment for dead and stinky trout, which mine lacks. You pick your own contrivance.

I stuff lightweight waders and brogues into the daypack. The wading belt that holds my waist pack also carries a Folstaf in its holster. I don't use the staff often but bless it whenever it saves my life, which seems to be once or twice a year. I store a water bottle in a pocket of the daypack because I fish the desert a lot. Another pocket holds a pair of sunglasses, a floppy hat that I picked up on a trip to New Zealand, and a windbreaker that I bought for a trip to windy Chile but use constantly in our windier West.

Another pocket of my daypack holds what I guess could be called a medical kit: sunscreen; a snakebite kit—the real thing, not whiskey; mosquito repellent; bandages; a small flashlight for those days when trout detain me until after dark; pills for headaches when I get outfished by my friends; and a waterproof fire starter kit, which I consider a necessity though I've not yet been forced to use it. I think that's all, but I'm sure I've forgotten to list something that you should remember and put into your own condensed kit.

After the last trip, when I forgot them, I added a pair of wool socks to keep my feet warm when wading cold water and a set of Polypro underwear to wear under my waders because jeans or khaki pants are cold, uncomfortable, and emerge wet with sweat. But those are clothes and might or might not be considered fishing gear. If you have room in your pack, include them so you don't forget them like I did.

I originally packed this kit for frequent day trips to my home Deschutes River. As it turns out, I use the daypack and double rod tube to outfit myself for trips as far as Montana. Last year, I carried the combination on a speaking swing to fishing clubs in North Carolina and Missouri, where it turned out I needed nothing I didn't have in the daypack and had some of my best fishing of the year.

I should never confess that I once took no more fishing gear than a couple pack rods and what fit in the old blue daypack on a three-week trip to Patagonian Chile. I felt lightened by the absence of all the gear I'd left at home and did not miss any of it on the entire trip. Freedom and comfort can reside at times more in a little than a lot.

28

Spike Camping
For Fly Fishing

Spike camping provides a special set of satisfactions. It sets you down where fishing is far better than it is for those unfortunate folks you've left behind. But don't feel sorry for them. You'll earn that sense of separation. You'll have to carry your own camp.

A spike camp is the lightest and smallest gathering of gear you can hoist and hike away with and still feel safe from the surrounding elements. Your goal, whenever you spike out, is freedom to fish. You achieve it by carrying less equipment, not more. I'll give you an example.

My friend Jim Schollmeyer and I fished a remote stream in the mountains of eastern Oregon out of a beautiful campground last summer. Trouble was, the campground was full. Everybody started out in the morning from the same point, with the same destination: upstream where the water was least fished and therefore the trout fishing was best.

Each day became a race that was impossible to win. If we dropped out to fish awhile, others sped on and fished the water in front of us. If we kept going to keep the lead, we got to the most distant and therefore the very best water with too little time left to fish it. We were forced to turn around and scoot in order to get back to camp before dark.

Jim and I solved this problem the next morning. We packed a small tent, sleeping bags and pads, some slight food and cooking gear, and headed out with all the others. We lazed along, dropped our packs, and fished while everybody else rushed ahead. In late afternoon, we arrived where everybody else had turned back. That's where we set our tent in the grass alongside the stream. We'd had an excellent day, spent fishing rather than racing. Then we spent the long and pleasant evening exercising trout while all the others spent it scooting downstream to get back to the campground before dark.

We fished upstream from our tiny spike camp the next two days. I won't bother you with the details about how well we did, except to tell you we caught lots of nice trout and didn't see another angler. We left each morning long before anybody else had time to get up that far, and we got back to our own tiny camp long after they'd all been forced to turn around at the ends of tethers that were staked to that distant campground.

A spike camp, by definition, is a small outcamp set some distance from a larger base camp. It's most common to spike away from a base camp that is set up near your vehicle. But a spike camp is not restricted to any set of original circumstances. You can spike out from a horse camp, motorboat camp, touring kayak camp, or any other kind of camp.

A few years ago, I got struck by the desire to explore the river flowing into the head of a desert reservoir. No roads approached within miles of the reservoir's remote upper end. A wheel-rut road touched the lower end at the dam. I drove there, launched a canoe, and spent a long, lazy day dipping my paddle at the right speed to troll a streamer. This gained me a few bursts of excitement during the pleasant day, and also a few fat trout fillets to grill over a campfire in a base camp that I set up at the head of the reservoir that evening, right next to where the river came in.

Coyotes prowled around the tent and sneaked off with the remains of those trout that night. I interrupted their morning howl the next dawn by emerging from my base tent with a small pack on my back. I hiked half a day upstream, set up a spike camp, and spent a day and a half discovering that the upper river carried an absurd load of smallmouth bass that rarely got pestered, along with a scattering of rainbow trout that had grown to good size in all that loneliness. Such news never seems to disappoint me.

Though a spike camp officially originates from a larger base camp, you'd be foolish to limit its use to that circumstance. You'll often improve your fishing by carrying the barest essentials for a camp in your vehicle, your drift boat, or your canoe. Hike away from the farthest point your main transportation can deliver you, without erecting a base camp, and set up your small camp wherever you find the best fishing. It's not truly a spike camp then, but the extra fish you catch by getting away from other anglers will never scold you for violating the definition of spike camping.

I assembled the minimum gear for a spike camp long ago and keep it in a small backpack at all times, ready to grab and go without worry that I'm forgetting something vital. I use it often to get into better angling from a base camp. I use it just as often to get away from places where others can drive a rig or row a boat, without ever bothering to build a base camp.

The goal of spike camping is freedom. It's best served by paring excess, not by carrying it. But I like a tent. I always envy those who set up camp with no more than a light nylon fly for shelter, so they can feel the campfire and see the stars. I enjoy the fire and the stars too, but either I'm far more frightened of snakes than they are, or I spend a lot more time in country where creatures live that prowl at night and wag their tails.

I know those stories about rattlesnakes crawling into sleeping bags for warmth are old wives' tales. If believing them makes me an old wife, I'll accept that and set up my tiny tent. Add a pad, sleeping bag, a change of underwear and socks, a set of Polypro long underwear, and you've got about all you really need to keep warm, dry, and safe from snakes for a short trip, unless it's winter, when you need more clothes but will find fewer snakes.

It helps to have food. I carry granola premixed with powdered milk, each breakfast in a separate Ziploc bag to which I just add water. A single brick of Trapper's Oat Bread, from a recipe found in *Camp Cooking* by Bill and Jo McMorris, supplies sufficient fuel for lunch. A few Power Bars will do the same. For dinners, I carry packages of Pasta Roni or Rice-A-Roni, to which I usually add a 6-ounce tin of canned chicken or turkey.

It takes a small pot to build the dinners, and I'll confess to carrying a small frying pan and a film canister filled with butter in case a trout defends itself fatally and I'm forced to eat it. That's about it for food. If it's the height of fire season, I also carry a backpacking stove and a pint of fuel. Most times, I omit the stove and cook over a fire of sticks burnt to a bed of coals.

Never neglect to carry a map, compass, and knife when you're out in the wilds. Add stick matches, a cigarette lighter, and fire starter cubes, all in something waterproof. A few years ago, I was on an October float trip down the Yellowstone River when an arctic storm smacked. I spiked out, was comfortable, and took a photo of my snowbound tent in the morning. Later I learned that two elk hunters, who had matches but nothing else with which to start a fire, were found frozen in the hills above the river about the time I snapped that photo of my tent. They had died the same night.

Water purification tablets prevent too many disasters to be omitted. I never trust the water anymore, anywhere. If it's possible to boil it or filter it with something like a First Need, that's best, but boiling takes time and a filtration system adds weight. Those little tablets have never let me down, and I never leave them home. The new drinking bottles with filtration built right in let you fish all day without carrying extra water.

Don't spoil your spike camp by carrying an overload of fishing gear. Use the suggestions in chapter 24 to assemble a minimum kit that contains everything you need and no extra.

A spike camp, whether it's set up from a base camp or from a base of transportation, can deliver you to more than excellent angling. A lot of what we angle for is exploration. There's no better way to explore than to first separate yourself from those places where most folks are willing to travel.

Last fall, I drove my four-wheel-drive pickup into one of the most beautiful meadows I've ever seen. It was moguled by an ancient glacier, grown to grass, cropped by elk and mule deer. A willow-lined stream threaded the meadow, flagged it with red and yellow leaves, brightened it with the sound of bounding water. The first night of the trip, I slept in the canopy of the pickup.

I woke up early the next morning, hiked downstream a couple hours, then fished back up to the rig the rest of the day. It would be ungraceful to complain about the fishing. Trout, all of them wild rainbows, were eager for my dry flies. But something was missing. It was obvious that other fishermen had driven to the same meadow, taken the same path downstream, angled back up, had the same great luck catching trout. It was all beautiful. Nobody else was around that day. But they could drive right up like I did. Somebody else might arrive at any instant.

The next day, I added breakfast, lunch, and dinners for three days to my perpetual pack. I left that gorgeous meadow and hiked upstream toward where no roads came within miles of the stream. I followed the stream all morning, sometimes wandering away from it, but always returning to it. I found a trail at first, but it didn't deliver me very far upstream.

In early afternoon, the streamcourse flattened and entered a broad glacial gorge, open and bemeadowed in the bottom. The trail petered out because whatever animals walked it, mostly deer and elk, were able to scatter and amble wherever they wanted. I could do the same, so naturally I arrowed straight to the stream and set up my spike camp in a copse of cottonwood trees. That took all of half an hour, after which I was free to fish and explore for the three days that my food held out.

I might have stayed as long as I liked, so long as I liked to eat trout, because fishing was as good as it gets, and the trout were almost overpopulated in that remote piece of stream. But such great fishing was not the main point. Fishing had been good enough right down by the rig. It was truly not that much better up in the remoteness of that carved canyon.

What was better was the beauty and the exploring. The stream was born almost full-voiced out of the loose gravel of a giant glacial cirque that served as a gathering basin. I glassed for deer with my miniature binoculars and spotted lots. Patches of quaking aspen high on the rims gleamed golden in the sunshine. I had the feeling I was seeing things that were not only beautiful, but rarely seen by others.

I spent three days in that canyon. I cast dry flies over small pools and drew up swift trout. I lazed around my spike camp, built fires and burned them down to coals, and cooked trout on them because trout were so abundant it would never hurt their population to connect my life to theirs in that way. I had time to read Tolstoy's first short novel, *The Cossacks*, set in mountains similar to the ones I was in, of current interest because the book is about Russians fighting futily with Chechen braves a century and a half before the present variation of the same battle over the same soil.

The entire time I was there in that canyon, along that little stream, I had a sense of separation from all the rest of the world. I didn't bother feeling sorry for all those who'd never see that beautiful place, enjoy that excellent fishing. I earned it. I carried my spike camp there on my back.

29

Applied Mountain Biking

I don't know anything about the technical aspects of mountain biking; I just know it delivers me to great fishing I would not otherwise enjoy. At times I beat up the bikes. All too often I get beat up by them. But some applications gain me rides that are almost as pleasurable as the fishing I'm after when I'm on them.

Logging companies have gated off most of the inactive forest roads that lead to my home streams in Oregon, where I pester cutthroat trout. It's a trend all across the continent: roads locked up on account of liability problems. But few companies mind if you ride a bike on those serene old roads. You're neither dangerous nor in danger, so you're not going to sue them.

You can't predict the sights that you'll see while mountain biking to a stream—I once startled a bobcat intent on separating a doe from her fawn—but one thing is fairly certain: When you set out under your own power, you're going to have the water to yourself when you arrive. My favorite cutts, left all alone, have grown fat and happy since those gates got locked, which doesn't displease me.

You can still apply your bike to fishing where backroads—or main roads, for that matter—are open to driving. Just hide your bike or lock it to a tree at the upper end of the stretch of stream you're going to fish for the day, then drive down to where you want to start. Fish upstream to the bike, pedal downhill to your rig, and head for home. This works especially well where an oxbow takes the river away from the road, then brings it back. If anybody accuses you of being lazy for riding rather than walking back to your rig, tell them you're saving the terrible wear gravel causes on felt soles.

At some lakes and ponds, in my home area and many others around the West, blockades have been built or trenches dug across access roads to keep motorized vehicles out. The reasons are various—to reduce fire danger, keep people from dumping trash, whatever—but my reasons for riding a mountain bike into these places are always the same: solitude and excellent angling.

I often use my bike for the shuttle rig on float trips. It can save a substantial shuttle fee, or the time spent shuffling rigs before you launch, or a long and tiring hike when you're finished fishing. My home Deschutes River has gravel roads along many of its best stretches. A 2- or 3-mile day float allows me to work the far, and therefore less fished, shore. I lock my bike at the ramp at the lower end if I'm with a companion or simply carry the bike in the drift boat if I'm alone.

I won't describe in detail the time I lashed my mountain bike upright in a whitewater raft and dashed through Wreck Rapids on a trip down the Deschutes. I came out of the rapids with my gunwales awash. The only things rising above the waterline were my head and shoulders and the handlebars of my bike. Folks observing from shore couldn't see the boat beneath me and thought I'd tried to pedal a bike down the rapids.

Adventures like that are not as rare as I'd like. My best friend and I have a small stream we like to visit no more than once a season, because of all the difficulty involved, along with the occasional danger. It's a long ride in, so we carry the rudiments of a camp in our saddlebags and stay overnight.

The road has been abandoned for decades. It is steep, overgrown with grass and tag alders, booby-trapped with moss-covered stones. There's a branch of the stream to cross; the bridge washed out eons ago. It looks like it would be easy to splash right across the shallow stream, but for some reason, we've yet to make it across without one or the other of us toppling into the water, which makes it fine spectator sport for the other.

Once, on the way back down that steep and overgrown road, after a couple days of great trout fishing, I was leading, fairly sailing, head low over the handlebars and ass high in the air over the seat, dodging stones and feeling agile. A mother ruffed grouse lined her brood of balls of fluff up behind her and emerged from the grass a few feet ahead of my flying front tire. Rick was hot on my rear. The roadside was a picket fence of fatal jackpines.

I laid the bike on its side, skidded to a stop within inches of the chicks. Rick stopped a foot or so from running over me. That placid gang of grouse ambled off, pecking at insects, as if these things happened every day and had gotten to be tedious.

Fitting out a mountain bike for fishing is easy. Just add a back rack and saddlebags, if it doesn't already have them. When I carry two-piece rods, I keep them in the rod tube and tie the tube to the main frame of the bike. The end sticks out under the handlebars, over the front wheel, and it's out of the way. When you make a turn, the tube stays straight, and surprisingly enough, that's very disconcerting, because your perception of the turn depends on seeing your front wheel angle in the direction you aim to go. When the rod tube stays straight, you get the idea you're going to go straight as well, and it takes a while to get used to the idea that the rod tube is not in charge of navigation.

In recent years, I've been buying nothing but four-piece travel rods because they're handy for traveling by air and they cast as well as two-piece rods. The short tubes for pack rods can be bungee-corded to the rack behind the bike seat, in which case they'll stick out over the stern but be out of the way as well as out of sight.

Saddlebags strapped to the bike will hold your waders and minimum kit or vest. If I'm on an all-day jaunt, I'll carry a small daypack for lunch, water bottle, folding wading staff, and camera. My daypack has wand pockets along the sides. I don't know what wands are—I think they're used by folks who abuse themselves on mountains rather than in streams—but I know that a short rod tube can be slipped into one of these pockets and tied off so that it rides out of the way.

I've discovered that the lightest of float tubes, inflatable by mouth, plus a set of breathable waders and a pair of swim fins can all be rolled up and strapped to the bike rack without causing much extra huffing on the way to a lake or pond. It's well worth all the freedom you'll gain when you get to a pond or lake others cannot reach by rig.

I know a favorite reach of stream where I can enter the water at the downstream end, on an abandoned spur road, fish upstream about 4 rugged miles, then exit the stream on another spur and hike back up to the main road. That main connecting road strays miles away from the stream. I fished this stretch the first time, years ago, without a bike and had a weary two-hour plod, about 6 miles, back to my rig after several brutal hours on the stream.

Fishing that gorgeous water was worth any effort, so I drove right back, but with my mountain bike. The country is so remote I didn't bother hiding the bike at the end of the upstream spur. I just wheeled it to the edge of the gravel and tipped it gently into thick brush where nobody would notice it if by small chance anybody drove by. The bike landed on a yellowjacket nest.

I stood still for a while, gazing forlornly at the angry insects buzzing and growling around the bike. Then I bit the bullet, because I wanted to get it over with while I was fresh enough to run, which I knew I would not be when I finished fishing. I pulled on heavy gloves, bloused my pant legs into my boot tops, tied a bandanna around my neck, and waded in.

All went well until three of those nasty yellowjackets bored beneath my hat and took turns trying to scalp me. I ran down the road waving the bike in the air and screaming for help until I finally gathered enough sense to toss the bike bouncing and throw off my hat.

Sometimes you carry the bike; most of the time the bike carries you, right to better fishing.

30

The Value of Revisitation

Some folks constantly bound off to find new fishing, always assuming it will be better where they're going because it's not very good where they've been. This kind of thinking is excellent when fishing is truly bad. But it becomes a self-fulfilling prediction on water where the fishing could be excellent if only they'd stick around, fish the same place twice.

By running all over the piscatorial landscape, we fail to harvest the advantage accrued by learning something about where we've been. I thought about this during a minor incident while fishing Oregon's McKenzie River with Scott Richmond, author of the acclaimed *Pocket Ghillie.*

Scott had floated the river a couple days earlier with his publisher, Madelynne Sheehan. The sun was out their day. March brown mayflies hatched but were scattered, but a hatch of caddis brought trout to the surface. Scott and Maddie had such an exciting time that Scott wanted to get right back, so he invited me to return to the river with him two days later, while Maddie stayed in the office to work on somebody else's book.

A storm struck our day. The march brown hatch died; no caddis ever appeared; the trout stayed down. Scott grumbled something about the kind of luck I brought, but he rowed the drift boat downstream because once you're launched, there are not many other directions you can go. We fished but failed to catch anything. An astounding downpour ended just as we entered the long flat upstream from the launch ramp that was our exit off the river.

I was eager to quit, but Scott angled the boat toward the other side of the river and anchored just upstream from a limb protruding from the water. It was the only feature on the flat. That whole region of river looked lifeless and fishless to me.

"Make a few casts to that limb," Scott ordered. "Maddie brought up three fish right there the day before yesterday."

I lofted some line, aimed at the limb, and set a downstream wiggle cast onto the water about 10 feet upstream from it. My March Brown Compara-dun drifted down attractively enough, but I had no confidence in the cast because no fish had arisen to appreciate any earlier cast, all day, which is probably why I was so surprised when a trout smacked the fly that I jerked back and broke it off.

"Good cast," Scott applauded, as if I'd just done something right rather than something wrong.

"Thanks," I said. I tied on a new fly and made the same cast. Another trout rose just as the dry drifted downstream to within a foot of the limb. I set the hook gently, played the trout carefully, and was about to land it when the hook came unpinned. I sat down and said, "Your turn."

Scott cast and caught one. We both tried for a while after that, but three trout were apparently that spot's allotment. The only fish we coaxed to the fly that day came because Scott remembered Madelynne had taken three fish in that spot, in that way, a couple days earlier.

One of my favorite nameless streams near my old home in Astoria has a pool that is far larger than those upstream and down from it. The stream whisks down a rocky riffle and enters the pool, bumps against a dark rock wall, and turns to flow along the face of the wall for 20 feet before rushing off into the next riffle. Right where it turns against the rock wall, the pool is 5 feet deep, which on a stream its size is the abyssal and dark depths.

I got a hint of what might lurk down there one day when I tossed my usual dry fly to the surface, drew up the usual couple of 8- and 9-inchers, then saw a flash deep under my fly. It was a big flash, though big is always relative to the size of where it happens.

I fished the rest of the way up to my rig that day, through a wonderful green forest, catching lots of cutthroat trout, not one more than 10 inches long. That was average, and I was far from disappointed. I drove away happy, but I also drove back a couple days later armed with something secret.

I inserted myself along the stream a half mile downstream from the big pool. I fished my way up toward it slowly, as I always do, casting dry flies and coaxing quite a few 8- to 10-inch trout, as I also always do. That was still average, and I suppose it's a fault of mine that I'm always pleased by the average when it's surrounded by beauty.

When I arrived at that deep pool, I pulled from my pocket a small-stream secret that my friend, fly-fishing author Skip Morris, taught me. It was simply a size 10 black nymph tied with several turns of weighting wire wrapped around its fuselage, along with a tuft of yellow yarn for an indicator to tie 4 feet up the leader from it. I nipped off my dry fly and assembled all this surreptitious gear. I passed the lower part of the pool without casting, therefore bypassing all the average trout, and aimed my first cast to deliver the nymph right where the riffle inserted itself at the head of the pool and rushed toward that turn. By the time the weighted nymph reached the deep place where the current butted against the cliff, it dangled down in the deep water where I'd seen that flash a couple days earlier.

I won't bother you with the rest of the story, except to say that the 14-inch trout was a monster for the stream from which it was extracted and to which it was quickly returned.

I have a habit of returning to a pond that is not far into the Coastal Mountains from my home in Portland. The leeward shore is a jackstraw tangle of fallen, floating logs. Their tops are bleached by exposure to the sun. Some are so stout it's easy to hop onto them and hike along their backs, far out into the pond, to use them as casting platforms. Others are slender. To step onto these is to engage in some brief and brisk log rolling, then a headlong pitch into the murk.

One day I log-hopped safely out toward open water, but just before I got there, I made an idle cast from a sturdy log over another I dared not walk and placed my fly back into a long, narrow gap between a couple other floating logs. My dry sat a moment, then disappeared in a boil outsize for the water it sat on. I was not prepared for this event. I played the trout for a few minutes with my line held high over one log and scraping along the side of another. The trout tired, but I was not able to lead it out of that gap, nor could I get safely to the gap to land it.

I drew the trout to the surface and tried to tug it, flapping, over the log that separated us. But the trout broke the frayed leader and slid back into its gap between the logs.

It didn't take any brilliance to return a week later and cast a dry fly tied to a stouter tippet down the length of that same gap between two logs. A small streamlet entered the pond nearby and brought the only cooling current. So I suspected that the large trout would not have moved. But it did not rise to that or to any of a frantic flurry of subsequent casts.

I wandered off, fished the rest of the pond, did quite well on trout of lesser size. It's a beautiful place, and you know I was happy. But my thoughts kept returning to that gap between logs. Then my mistake leaped suddenly before me: I'd sent the first cast sailing down the length of the narrow gap, therefore lining the whole thing. If that trout was still down there, I'd spooked it.

An hour later, I sneaked back, knelt as near as I could, and cast an Olive Woolly Bugger a leader length into that gap. I waited awhile, retrieved the cast slowly, and extended the next cast another leader length. Five casts later, you know what happened—all except the part where I timed a jump and flew the trout over the log on 3X tippet. It landed on my side with a smack, and the hook came free. But still I had the victory of having outsmarted it, or so I think, and the thrill of seeing it flying through the air at the end of my line.

It's surprising how often fishing improves when you return to water that beat you up a little the first time you fished it. I'm not knocking the urge to gallop off elsewhere when fishing is not excellent where you're at. But I am recommending an option to the idea. Try returning to a place where you've had just average fishing, especially if it's beautiful. Because of what you know about it the second time around, fishing will automatically be better. After that, you'll be attracted back and back. You'll learn a little more, and perhaps catch a few more or larger fish, at each revisitation. That's how home streams, and even lakes or ponds, get built.

31

The Angling Pace

Marcelo Dufflocq and I fished back-to-back up the wadable center of his unusual and gorgeous River of Swans, near Estancia de los Rios Lodge in Chile, where he is part owner and head guide. The stretch of river we fished was about a cast and a half across, with its holding water pushed up against bunchgrass banks on both sides. It was not normal in that most of the water was of relatively even depth all the way across. The best way to fish it was to get out away from the banks and cast in toward them, usually quartering upstream and across with a dry fly or nymph.

The trout were all browns. They took on the surface or under it with such boldness that we were never in doubt something had happened out there. We had no trouble knowing when it was a good time to set the hook.

I wouldn't use this Chilean example except that if you sliced Marcelo's river in half down its length, it was just about like so many of ours, where you wade or walk a shallow inside edge and cast across to deeper holding water pushed by the current to the outside edge. The only difference was that Marcelo and I were able to wade the center and cast toward opposite banks. In places, we had to be careful that our backcasts didn't quarrel.

Holding lies were not equally dispersed on both sides of the stream. For a hundred feet or a hundred yards, he might be casting toward the outside bend, where the current worked the banks and good lies would be denser. Then the current might shrug my way and offer a concentrated line of boulders sprinkled beneath those bunchgrass clumps and submerged to excellent depth, and I'd have the better water.

Marcelo's pace and mine varied with the quality of whatever water we fished at any instant. One of us would be ahead for a while, but before long, the other would wade past and never need to ask, "How are you doing?" because we were always in sight of each other. I had no trouble, for example, discerning that Marcelo, nicknamed the Cormorant from his youth for his ability to catch trout, got detained about twice as often as I did by the need to play out and release a trout. Sometimes I stopped casting for a few moments just to watch him getting splashed all around by a 2- or 3-pound brown and to feel sorry for him.

I hadn't fished for quite a while. My angling energies had been pent up by the northern winter. It was the first day of the trip and I landed at a lope. Marcelo moved along at the same pace, I think because he has spent years exploring waters across the vast Patagonian landscape, and his fishing has become part propellant to see what's around the next bend. That's a lot of what motivates me. I fish faster than my best interests, measured in terms of the numbers of trout held in my hands, would seem to dictate.

Over a half kilometer of river, we fished the same amount of bank, ended up at the jeep at the same time for the bounce back to the lodge for dinner, and except for that imbalance in trout caught, we fished with an equality of enjoyment and at the same pace. It's a pleasure to fish with somebody who seems to be around whenever you need confirmation for a success or sympathy for a failure, yet is never between you and any water you'd like to fish.

Marcelo is the only person I've fished with who makes way at the same pace I do when my motor gets revved up. He also has a fine guide's ability to adjust his pace to whomever he is with, and when he is guiding, he does not fish at all, which I think must be the ultimate test of anybody's ability to adjust his fishing pace. I lack that sort of patience; you would not want to be guided by me. Nor would you want to fish at my pace.

Your fishing pace should be adjusted to suit your own personality and to balance your desires to cover water and see new things against the slightly conflicting desire to capture more trout. If you're a disciplined, methodical, perhaps even phlegmatic person, you should do your fishing at a studious, patient pace. You won't enjoy it any other way. If you fished with me and tried to keep up, when we got together for lunch you'd accuse me of leaving you in the dust and trampling all the good water before you got a chance to fish it. You'd be right; I apologize.

At the same time, I'd be a bit peeved for the number of times I had to rein myself in and hike back over water I'd already fished to see if you were still coming along. We wouldn't do well fishing together unless we found some way to split up the stream. Which is a way of saying that your own pace, after it's adjusted to suit yourself, should be somewhat in sync with whomever you're on the stream with on a given day.

I fished one day on the same river with a group of four clients from Minnesota. They'd spent a lot of time fishing together, but never on a big river. Two of them hit the water and whapped their way right along it. Their guide had to run to keep them in sight. In an hour and a half, they'd reached the jeep at the upper end of the designated stretch for the entire morning. Then they sat and fumed while they waited for their friends. One of the gentlemen set out at a patient pace, covered all of the water all the way up to the jeep, and arrived there just in time to head in to the lodge for lunch. He did very well and loved that stretch of river.

The fellow I was with inserted himself into the loveliest run he'd ever seen in his life and hoisted half a dozen trout out of it that were a pound or so each. He was so enthralled with where he was that he ignored me when I told him we had a lot of water to cover to get upstream to our ride. He spent more than three hours fishing 100 feet of stream. I didn't feel good about leaving him, so I sat and read a paperback while he fished. When it finally became time to go, he waded out and we walked all the way up to the jeep together, alongside the river, more than a mile in a hurry to catch our ride in for lunch.

"There's a lot of good water up here that we didn't get a chance to fish," he told me as we huffed and hiked. It sounded a lot like it was my fault. Later on in the trip, the four of them figured out the best pace for the river and for each other. All but one had to make substantial changes in the speed, or lack of it, with which they fished the water.

You're going to be most compatible fishing with other folks who move at about the same pace you prefer. If you notice that you're having fun lingering on the same bit of water for an extended length of time and that you're catching a number of trout that is satisfying to you, it's still necessary to notice if your partners are spending most of their time sitting on the bank watching you. That does not mean angling has evolved into a spectator sport for them, that you're doing so well and doing it so attractively that they prefer watching you to fishing themselves. It's more likely to mean that they're waiting for you to finish and move on with them so they can get back to their own fishing without feeling guilty for leaving you behind. Idle companions are often a sign that you should pick up the pace: skip some water or fish it faster.

If the opposite is true—you find yourself sitting on the bank tying nail knots that don't need replacing—then you could contribute to solving the situation by tugging at the handbrake a bit, covering water somewhat more slowly. Chances are, though, that if you find yourself either watching or being watched, you're not going to enjoy each other's companionship until you find a way to split up the stream.

Leapfrogging pools, the old standard way to apportion good water, will drive you both nuts if you fish at dramatically disparate paces. You'll rarely find water that you can slice down its length and share back-to-back, the way Marcelo and I did. The best way to split a stream and share it comfortably with somebody who fishes at an awkward pace for you is to separate, go to different sections, fish in the pleasantry of your own company, then meet back at the jeep, boat, airplane, or whatever conveyed you to the water you're sharing. Then you can take time to trade lies about the trout you caught before bolting or meandering off to fish further separate sections.

Setting the right speed for yourself, and then adjusting it for whomever you're with, solves two parts of this problem of pace. The third and perhaps most important is adjusting your pace to the water you're on. It might be smart to move briskly along a tiny stream, showing your fly just a few times at each likely pool. If you get into a broad riffle or run on a larger river and try to cover it in the same amount of time, with the same number of casts, you're not likely to catch nearly as many trout. Your movement might be fast, but when you're done, you'll declare that fishing was slow.

I'm not implying here that you should count the casts you make. You just must learn to adjust your pace to the density of likely lies in any given stretch of water and make the number of casts it takes to show your fly to any trout within those lies. Every trout in a small-stream pool might see your fly on the first four or five casts. In a broad riffle or run, it might require several times that many casts, with each drift of a dry, tumble of a nymph, sweep of a streamer or wet fly covering its separate foot or two of water, before you're satisfied that all possible trout have had a chance to accept or reject whatever it is you're offering.

Perhaps that is the most valuable angling asset acquired by fly fishermen with as much experience as Marcelo Dufflocq: their ability to size up a certain stretch of water, then fish it at the pace that best suits their personality, that of their companions, and the water over which they're casting.

32

Fly Selection Simplified

When you peel all the peripheral layers of the problem out of your way, trout-fly selection reduces itself to a simple set of just three steps. Separate these, focus on them in the correct order, and each leads to the solution of the next. You'll end with a fly tied to your tippet that catches trout.

Before getting to the three steps, let me note that you should always initiate your trout-fly selection only after you've stepped to streamside and looked around. Don't park your rig, tug on your waders, and decide right there, without sight of the stream, what fly you're going to fish. I'll embarrass myself with an example of what happens when you make that mistake.

My wife and I recently drove to a small stream near home. It was late spring, and we were eager to get out after confinement by a few days of rain. I knew the water would be high. My vast experience prodded me to string up a weighted nymph and strike indicator, right at the rig, so I could fish deep under streamy current tongues, where I knew all the trout would be holed up.

I dropped down to the stream on a deer trail and immediately began nymphing upstream from pool to small pool. I left Masako in my wake, sitting on a streamside rock, eating a sandwich and contemplating conditions. The stream was brisk and a bit swollen, but my indicator had already dipped three or four times by the time she caught up with me a few pools later. I'd caught a couple of trout. I was proud about my success and surprised to see that she, having noticed a scant two or three golden stoneflies in the air, had tied on a big Stimulator dry.

"I doubt you'll do much with that today," I warned her before she stepped around me to the next pool. She set that brushy fly accurately onto a tiny pocket of eddied water off to the side of the main current where I'd have fished. Somebody should have warned the trout. One rushed up and impaled itself on her dry.

Masako led three trout to her hands in that one pool, by casting her dry fly onto the edges and eddies rather than the main currents. She worked her way upstream ahead of me, dancing more trout, while I frantically stripped that nymph and indicator off my leader so I could rerig with a dry like hers. She had followed the steps that led her to the correct fly selection. I had not. Let me parse them out here, since I obviously need a refresher myself.

The first step at streamside is to observe conditions and interpret them into the type of fly—dry, nymph, wet, or streamer—it is best to fish. Take notice of wind and weather conditions, air and water temperatures, whether the water is high and muddy, low and clear, or somewhere on the continuum between. It's not necessary to measure anything. Just take time to gather a rough idea about how things look and feel to you and assess how active or inactive trout might be in the water, at this moment.

Look for trout. If you see them—rising, cruising, winking along the bottom—well, there they are. You'll know what type of fly will reach them at the depth they're feeding, because you can see them. Advance to the next step and choose the right pattern to catch them.

In the absence of visible trout, look for insects, even if they're few and not on the water. When insects are flying over water that is not so deep that trout would not bother rising all the way to the top—usually 2 to 4 feet—or so dirty that they can't see to the top, it's probably a dry-fly day. A hackled searching dry, such as a Royal Wulff or Elk Hair Caddis, will likely draw trout up.

If you see insects over and on water that is the same somewhat shallow depth, but you see no fish rising, try fishing a traditional wet fly, or a brace of them, on the swing in the mid-depths. It's an old but still excellent way to cover lots of water—step and cast, step and cast down riffles, runs, and pools. Wets work best when it seems trout should be feeding on top but they're not.

If the air is cold, the water is cool and looks lifeless, and no insects are out and about, your choices dip down to the bottom. You might try a streamer fished deep in pools or swept across tailouts. In shallow riffles and deeper runs, tie on a nymph, adding split shot to get it down and a strike indicator to relay news about takes.

I'll give you a bold summation about fly type here: The most successful trout fishermen I know go directly to a nymph, split shot, and strike indicator setup unless specific indications, such as visible rising trout, dictate a different method.

Now that you know which fly type to try—dry, nymph, wet, or streamer—the second step, the critical decision, looms: Which particular fly to try? Most often, specific fly selection is easy, because you've already acquired enough hints to tell you what to use.

If a hatch is happening, collect a specimen in your hand or hat. Don't worry about its Latin name. Just observe its size, form, and color and match it as closely as you can. A couple of common errors are to go a size too large, when it's better to be right on or even a size too small, or to match the back color of the insect. The belly is nearly always a lighter color, and that's what trout see when they tip up to take a floating natural.

If conditions predict success with a dry fly but you see no hatch to match, notice if any insect is dominant, even if it's not on the water. Choose a dry fly close to it. That's what Masako did the day she noticed a few golden stones in the air, tied on a Stimulator, and abruptly outfished me.

If insects are out but none are dominant, choose a dry fly that averages them. If you have nothing else to go on, use a drab Adams, fished close, on somewhat smooth water; a buoyant Elk Hair Caddis, fished at medium range, on water that is bouncy;

or a bright Royal Wulff, still fished at close to medium range, on boisterous water. If, for any of these situations, you already own a favorite dry fly, be sure to use it.

If conditions look likely for a nymph, hoist a few rocks off the bottom and examine what might be clinging to them. If one insect species is dominant, match it as nearly as you can. If nothing stands out, try a nymph in a common size and color. My favorites are the Fox Squirrel and Olive Beadhead in size 14 or 16. Both look like lots of naturals. I often use a weighted Brook's Stone or Olive Scud in a larger size, then tie the smaller fly as the point. This offers trout a choice, always a good way to find out fast what fly will fool them.

If you choose a wet fly or streamer, don't worry much about which one unless a specific food form is active, in which case you should match it. But it's usually best if your sunk fly is fairly small, say size 10 to 14, and drab, in keeping with the colors of most natural food forms that trout eat. Most of the time you'll use these swimming flies to explore water, fishing downstream, probing everywhere, trying to entice scattered trout.

That condenses specific fly selection: If a food form is active and available, match it; if a variety of insects are out, approximate them with a dry on the surface or a nymph on the bottom. If no food forms are active, choose a proven searching dry, nymph, wet, or streamer, depending on the level you've chosen to fish, based on the observations you've already made.

The third and final step in fly selection is activated only if your chosen fly fails to fool trout. Put the brakes on your fishing; check to see if your original observations and interpretations still seem right. If they do, try a different fly in the same type: dry, nymph, wet, or streamer. Switch from a bright dry to a drab one, from a small nymph to a large one, from one wet or streamer to another.

Make just one or two changes of flies within a type, then switch from one fly type to another. If you've tried two or three drys of different sizes, shapes, and colors and none drew strikes, go to nymphs or some other sunk style. If trout refuse a few nymphs, try swinging a wet or streamer or tying on a dry fly.

Most often, if you observe what's happening on the stream and interpret it correctly, you'll choose the right fly in the first place. But keep in mind that conditions change all day, almost every day, and so does what works. Whenever your catch falls off, stop casting and take time to examine prevailing conditions. Notice what has changed and what you need to change in your fly pattern or way of fishing it to bump your success back up to where you deserve it to be.

33

Looking at Little Things

It's winter as I write this, but I'm tying flies based on a vial of insects I collected during a hatch last summer. The trout that provided the insects in the vial rose without discernible regularity but for a long time among many others on a smooth Deschutes River flat that broke over into a long and brutal riffle, the kind of rough-and-tumble water for which the Deschutes is more famous. This selective trout defied solution until I tied a size 18 Beadhead Prince as a dangler beneath a size 16 Parachute Adams. After having rejected nearly everything else in my fly boxes, the fish rushed the Prince the instant the fly touched the water. I'd like to report that it was the solution and end the story here, but it was not. I kept on pestering other rising trout on the same flat with the same fly, but all the others refused it.

I killed that fish. For those of you who are among the horrified, I feel bad for you, but it was a hatchery steelhead smolt that had become a resident trout rather than backing downstream to the ocean where it belonged. It needed to be removed from the gene pool before it passed on its habit of refusing to migrate, or so I rationalized my desire to have it for dinner and also examine its stomach to see what it had been eating.

I sat at a table on a deck at Redsides Retreat, next to the flat from which I'd extracted the trout that provided the stomach. I sliced the stomach open and squeezed its contents into a pickle jar lid that was white inside. I always keep that little lid in a vest pocket. It's the handiest thing I've found for an occasional examination of stomach samples.

The lid is also excellent and used more often when I collect the nymphal, larval, or pupal stage of an aquatic insect and desire a close look at it. When water is added to the jar lid, it provides a contrasting background against which the living natural can be seen clearly. The parts of the insect stand out, and the way it moves is evident. That might tell you a lot about the right fly pattern to fish for it, and also about the right way to fish that fly.

What the trout had eaten looked like olive-brown toothpaste in the jar lid until I added enough river water to fill the lid almost to the brim, then swizzled and poked at the mass with a pair of tweezers. The paste slowly separated out and resolved itself into, among other things, the insects in the vial from which I'm now tying flies.

If you have not done it, it's magic to see a stomach sample untangle and become evidence. At first, it all looks like goo. Then you add water and gently stir it until it begins to separate into recently eaten and little-decomposed insects mixed in with a soup of digested contents that were eaten earlier.

If the water becomes too cloudy from digested contents, carefully pour it off, add clean water, stir, pour, and add clean water again until only the least-digested insects remain. These become easy to examine against the white background of the jar lid. Though few will be in perfect condition, it will not be difficult to separate the individuals into types and to notice if any one species of insect predominates in the trout's recent diet.

The stomach contents in the jar lid I examined there on the deck next to the river included a few small beetles, some mayfly duns and caddis adults, plus a vast predominance of tiny midge pupae. I ignored the other things as aberrations of the sort that led the trout to its fatal encounter with the Beadhead Prince nymph and began tweezering the midge pupae into the vial of ethyl alcohol. As I did, the reasons for my defeat began to reveal themselves to me.

First, the midge pupae were all dark olive-brown, and I had no midge pupa patterns with me in anything but black, red, and tan. Second, the insects were all of a size that was smaller than anything I had on me that day. In one of my fly boxes, somewhere at home, I might have had a pattern that small, but I'd pared my luggage to the main boxes I always carry, which I've recommended but which can also at times be a mistake you should let me make but avoid yourself.

It's the peripheral small boxes that I scatter here and there in various wader bags, boat bags, and belt bags that contain my attempts to solve things I don't encounter often. I do not often have all of those boxes with me.

As I tweezered the midge pupae patiently from the jar lid to the vial, using my loupe to pick them out, I noticed that about half were well-formed pupae. The other half had been eaten in the process of extracting their wings from their pupal cases and turning into adults. These were emergers and had probably been taken struggling in the surface film. The pupae that preceded them likely got captured by the trout either on their way to the top or suspended just beneath the surface film.

That act of tweezering midges revealed that I was dealing with a trout that was at least somewhat selective, taking mostly olive midge pupae just beneath the surface film or olive midge emergers in the film itself. I can't say that I was surprised by any or all of this, but I will say that I was surprised by the clarity with which the problem resolved itself once I took time to examine it. I'd been flummoxed by trout on that same flat, doing that same thing, for some seasons, held back from analyzing the problem by my reluctance to kill a trout in order to obtain a stomach sample.

Another thing surprised me: Each movement I made to transfer an insect from the lid to the vial represented a movement to rise and take by the trout. I was patient. The trout had been far more patient. In the time during which I cast over it, assuming that all of its feeding got condensed into that time, which of course it did not, the trout came up and took a midge and went back down to its shallow lie between seventy-five and a hundred times. That, in my mind, represents a clear and determined focus

on getting fed, though I suppose that when I sit down at the dinner table, I scoop something with my spoon or stab something
with my fork around the same number of times. I'll count bites
tonight; you do the same.

Recognizing the shape and size and color and consistency of
the problem does not assure that the flies I'm tying now in winter will constitute any sort of solution next summer. My winter
tying amounts to guesses. I won't know how I've done until I
get back out on that flat when those midges happen again. Then
I'll fish what I've tied and see how I've done.

Meantime, I'll buy a separate small fly box with lots of little
compartments. I'll tie my guesses by the half dozen and drop
them into that box, and only that box. It's what I call an experimental fly box; I have them for *Baetis* and pale morning dun and
march brown mayflies, and for certain abundant caddis hatches.
The flies I tie for the midges will break down into two sets: one a
guess at the nicely formed pupae that were taken before they
began to emerge, the other based on the emergers that the trout
seemed to have taken on half of its rises.

I'll tie each fly in a narrow range of sizes. But that's only
because I'd like to see what the trout might accept in the way of
variation. The first thing I did when I sat down at the tying bench
was to tie a single pupal pattern on each hook size from 20 to 28.
Then I compared these flies directly with the real things in the
vial. Not until I reached size 28 did the imitations match the true
size of the naturals. As I tie by the half dozens now, it's with the
hope that trout will accept something slightly larger than the
naturals. However, I'll be able to offer them something precisely
right if they demand it.

It was mostly for my own benefit that I tied those flies in
descending sizes and compared them so closely to the real thing.
Now I know how often, and how easily, we misjudge size when
we select a pattern on the stream, in the confusion that is the
process of trying to catch a selective trout rising to something
that is almost invisible. I could have solved some of this problem by carrying a collecting net, but these insects were probably
small enough to have escaped through the mesh.

I won't tell you the patterns I'm tying. That wouldn't be fair,
because nothing is proved yet. I haven't tried them yet. I will tell
you that there are three steps to this process of puzzling out a

hatch, and that they're all fun. The first step is collecting and analyzing the insects. You need a minimal amount of tools to do it: a pickle jar lid, a pair of tweezers—mine are from a Swiss Army knife that I always carry anyway—and a 4X to 6X loupe, which I'm assigning you to carry if you're at all interested in the insects that trout eat.

The second step is the winter tying—summer if you've got the time, which I do not. This is the guessing you do, basing your ties on the observed size, form, and color of what you've collected, filling the compartments of that experimental fly box until you've got a comfortable number of options to try.

The third step is to go back out and go fishing during the same hatch. This might be the most fun of the three, but I'm not entirely sure about that. If you're the scientific type, you might enjoy the analysis most. If you're a dedicated tier, you'll get the most kick out of tying those options. I like the third part best because I'm happiest when I have my waders in trout water.

I can tell you how I'll rig to fish these flies on that flat. I'll use a size 18 Parachute Adams on 5X tippet for an indicator. I'll drop an emerger dressing off that on 6X. I'll dangle a pupal pattern off the stern of the emerger, on 6X or 7X, and in that way I will have offered the trout a choice. I'll make my presentations across stream or even downstream to the rising trout with a reach cast or wiggle cast. I'll spend a lot of time with all three flies tangled together if the Deschutes River wind is blowing, and I'll be fuming with impatience as I try to untangle them.

I predict that I'll catch only a few of the fish that are rising—in other words, that I'll solve only part of the problem. I don't expect any sort of overwhelming acceptance of any of the guesses I've made. And I predict that the trout will confound my experiment by taking the Parachute Adams almost as often as they take anything I've tied to match the midges. After all, the original pounce was made on a Beadhead Prince, which looks nothing at all like the midge pupae and emergers in that vial.

I predict that I'll catch a few more of those selective trout than I did last time, when I caught just one. And I predict that I'll come home with a few more experiments to make for next time. That's what I consider fly-fishing success: doing a little better than the last time you fished a hatch and being enthusiastic about what still needs to be tried next time.

34

When a Fly Is Not
What It Seems

Masako and I hiked the steep poplar trail to the first meadow of
Slough Creek, in Yellowstone Park, one bright July day. Everybody else had gone dashing on toward the second meadow or
had driven off to view bison and other beasts. The meadow was
surprisingly empty of anglers when we arrived in late morning.
Trout were already rising when we got there.

You always expect hoppers in summer on Slough Creek, but
these rises were dainty and almost invisible, not the forceful
swirls or minor detonations with which meadow stream trout
murder large terrestrial insects. Something smaller prompted
such subtle sips. It took only minor discipline—sitting in the
warm sunshine and watching the water while we slowly strung
our rods—to notice enough tiny *Baetis* mayfly duns in the air and
on the water to cause those cutthroat trout to concentrate their
feeding. The hatch was no blitz, but sufficient olives boated the
gentle currents to make it obvious what was happening. Or so I
thought.

Masako tied on a Little Olive Compara-dun and scurried
eagerly to the next pool downstream, certain she had a sudden

solution to the situation. I tied a size 18 René Harrop Hairwing Dun to a long 6X tippet and began casting to the nearest rises. I also expected instant success. That fly over that insect had proved itself often and almost without fail.

It failed finely that day. Those supposedly stupid cutts not only continued to rise around it, but refused even to swim over and refuse it. None looked at it. Of course, it's easy now, looking back, to understand that the trout were taking nymphs just as they approached the surface for emergence, so close to the top that they sent soft rise rings upward. But I was standing next to the stream with a fly rod in my hand and trout feeding right in front of me, not sitting at a desk chewing on the end of a pen and pondering the situation with the wisdom we call hindsight. My judgment wasn't clear, and I did something as stupid as what one of those native cutthroat was supposed to do but didn't.

I jerked the dry fly under in disgust and retrieved it toward me to replace it. You know a trout jumped it.

I played the trout out while Masako did her customary dance around me, shooting photos for her magazines in Japan. When I released the fish and showed her what I'd hooked it on—even gave one to her—I neglected to mention how I'd fished it. This was in part out of dishonesty, but in another part because I assumed it was an accident and the fly would still work as a dry.

I cast it again, fished it on the float again, and again got nothing. I tugged it under out of curiosity. Another trout took it on a slow, submerged swim. To condense the rest of the story, I told Masako the truth about the sunk retrieve, and we spent the afternoon catching trout happily ever after.

We've all caught trout that tipped up their noses at dry flies but took them as soon as they sank. I always consider it an accident—usually an unwanted one, because I'm unable to explain it. I think I fail to connect the accidental take with the reasons behind it. When it happens, trout are almost always taking the subsurface and invisible stage of whatever is emerging and visible on the surface.

Once that connection is considered and the appropriate softhackle, wet fly, or nymph is tied on, even selective trout that are not stupid cutts can become surprisingly easy.

The opposite can happen, as well. I once fished a pale morning dun hatch on the Bighorn River in Montana with Jim Schollmeyer, author of *Hatch Guide for Western Streams*. I wore out a pod of trout that were rising in some fairly fast water and caught enough on standard PMD Sparkle Dun drys to make me think I was good. When no more rose where I was, I reeled up and looked up and there was Jim, standing at the edge of a giant eddy with a deep bend in his rod. I walked up to applaud. Jim, ever generous with trout, told me to go ahead and cast over the gang of black noses poking through the surface all over that eddy.

I did. Nothing happened to the Sparkle Dun, which had moments earlier been a killer. Jim resumed casting next to me and almost instantly displaced me to make room to play another nice brown trout. I asked him what he was using.

"A Ginger Sparkle Pupa," he told me, "dressed and in the film." The trout, it turned out, were taking trapped pale morning dun cripples caught in the eddy. It seemed a dishonorable solution. Gary LaFontaine's Emergent Sparkle Pupa strides the border between wet fly and nymph. It is designed to be fished inches deep during caddis hatches. Jim fished it dry during a mayfly hatch. When dressed with floatant, the fly flopped on its side and was nothing but a tangle in the water. It looked a lot like a pale morning dun trapped in its nymphal shuck and the surface film at the same time.

I had nothing like that in my fly boxes. I started to whine, but Jim gave me one to shut me up before I ever got going. This book deserves a chapter on how to whine flies out of friends; it's such a critical skill, and I'm such an expert at it, but your friends deserve not to have it written.

A dry fished wet on Slough Creek and a wet fished dry on the Bighorn: You see where we're headed. If you fish a fly wrong, it's often the right solution to a situation in which you can find no normal match for a hatch.

I got into a damselfly migration once on a high desert lake but didn't know it right away. I had waded far out onto a shallow flat, toward some bold swirls I saw out there. This lake holds Lahontan cutts up to 5 and 6 pounds. I could not tell what they were eating. I tried size 12 Zug Bugs and Herl Nymphs, which usually work, and all sorts of other stuff that usually does not, the sort of thing you do when you're desperate. Once again, I got nothing but refusals from cutts that are supposed to accept anything.

I ceased my frantic casting long enough to watch the water awhile. A single green damselfly nymph struggled into sight in front of me, then spent what seemed like most of a week but was probably only a couple minutes swimming past me. I watched where it went and saw a boil that was its obituary.

My fly boxes were empty of damselfly nymph imitations but held an entire row of size 10 Olive Woolly Buggers—the fly box that does not could almost be considered empty. I plucked one out and pinched off all but a few hackles near the head, leaving a few that stuck out like whiskers or, I hoped, like the legs of a natural damsel. I thinned out the tail to no more than a wisp of marabou, tied this slenderized Woolly Bugger to my tippet, cast it out, and soon was able to punish the same trout that had so recently murdered the natural damselfly nymph.

Since that day, a barbered Olive Woolly Bugger has become my standard imitation for green damsels. The same fly when truncated at the tail end is an excellent dragonfly nymph dressing. I discovered that in about the same way. I caught a trout from a local lake that holds only planted trout, after a long time spent fishing a variety of flies fruitlessly. I whacked the trout to take home for dinner. Its stomach—never kill a trout without snooping into what it has been eating—contained two fat Aeschnidae nymphs.

Again, I had no match for them but had that row of size 10 Olive Woolly Buggers. I pinched the after half of the marabou tail off one, left the rest of the bulky fly intact, cast it out, let it sink, brought it back along the bottom with a patient hand-twist retrieve. Success was neither instant nor constant, but I drove home having had a lot more action than I'd have had without that minor application of a streamer to a nymph situation. It's become a standard procedure since then, whenever I fish a lake with a good population of those big hourglass-shaped aquatic insects: abbreviate a Woolly Bugger and fish it slow and deep as a dragonfly nymph.

Richard Bunse and I once floated Oregon's broad and placid Willamette River in his 12-foot drift boat. We got into a hatch of olives—*Baetis* again—that came off in a still backwater and lasted only an hour. That doesn't leave a lot of time to solve a situation, but when a brief hatch starts, you don't know in advance that it's also almost over.

Bunse tied on a size 18 Olive Compara-dun, as he almost always does, and while I tried to decide what to do, he caught a trout, which he also almost always does. Then I had a sudden inspiration. I recalled that day with Masako on Slough Creek when a dry fly fished wet worked so well. I had some size 16 Little Olive Flymphs in my *Baetis* box, and I decided to try the fur-bodied wets as nymphs swimming up for emergence. I tied one on, but it didn't work.

Trout ignored the wet fly on the swim. Bunse kept catching them on his dry. After a while, I cast the flymph out near the anchored boat and let it idle while I searched my boxes for an Olive Compara-dun—Bunse has unfortunately become immunized against my whining, once even told me he'd begun to enjoy it. I couldn't find the fly I wanted. While I looked, the fibrous flymph caught in the surface film and failed to sink. You know what happened next.

After releasing the first trout, I dried the wet fly on my handkerchief, dressed it with floatant, and proceeded to almost overtake Bunse. If that hatch had not ended so abruptly, I might have accomplished a rare feat and outfished him.

The hatch was the same as the one on Slough Creek. That time I fished a dry fly wet. This time I fished a wet fly dry. Who can explain trout? I cannot. I only know that if you keep your mind and your options open, you'll catch a lot more of them.

35

Insect Identification:
What Is a Useful Level?

Imagine that you desire to give yourself a single overarching assignment that will absorb your angling interest, increase your catch, and at the same time increase the pleasure you extract from the watery world in which trout abound. I advise you to take up in a minor way, or if it intrigues you as much as it does me, a more major way, the observation and study of the aquatic insects that trout make a living eating and that we make a catch by imitating.

Several levels exist to which you can take this study of insects. You're already at one of them if you're already out there fishing. You need do no more than gaze at what is going on around you, let some of it sink in. If you begin to swipe an occasional insect into your hat or hoist a rock from the streambottom and note what's on it, you advance your knowledge and increase your chances of catching trout.

This beginning bit of collecting serves two great purposes. First, it lets you relate your fly pattern selection to the very thing that trout are eating. Second, unless you're entirely uncurious, it will excite you about the complex world in which trout live.

Suddenly fly fishing is not so simple a formula as fisherman + fly = trout.

I know that sounds bad to some folks. I hear the old argument all the time from those who declare that the study of insects is harmful to fly fishing because it complicates what should be a simple sport. That is nonsense. The sport is not simple, or it would never hold our interest as it does. And the complexities are always there. It's nature, not we, that creates them. We have the choice to turn our backs on them or to look at them at different levels, according to our own interest.

Your increasing understanding of any complexity in the lives of trout, no matter how slight, will cause you to catch more of them. It also will make you more curious about the bugs and all other aspects of living streams and stillwaters. It will add to your fun whenever you're out fishing. If it doesn't, but instead gives you something to grump about, it probably means that you get your fun from grumping.

You don't need to acquire any equipment to accomplish that first level of collecting, but I hope it prompts you to take a simple next step to the next level of study, if you haven't already done it: Buy a $2 aquarium net to capture insects and a $10 4X to 6X loupe to have a closer look at them. The requirements in terms of time spent studying and equipment carried will be light, but the rewards might be heavy when held wet and dripping in your hands.

The first level of collecting will open your eyes to what's out there. This second level will let you begin to focus on the things that are important to you as an angler. I'll give you a small example of what I mean. For many years, I fished over a speckle-wing (*Callibaetis*) mayfly hatch on a local pond. I'd long ago caught a dun in my hat by thrashing pondside vegetation, noted its dominant tan and brown colors, adjusted my imitation, done well enough with it. But I didn't do as well as I'd have liked.

On a more recent trip, I lifted a dun off the water with an aquarium net, looked at it through my loupe, and tipped it upside down to observe its underside, which happens to be the side trout observe when they tip up to take one. That belly was far more pale than the back. It also contained some olive I'd not noticed earlier. I adjusted my pattern once again, and though I still don't catch as many trout as I see rising during that hatch, I catch a lot more than I did in the past.

The reason was not necessarily the net and the loupe. I could have done the same thing with my hat and naked eye. But with the net, I lifted a fresh dun off the water rather than sweeping a stale one, its exoskeleton already hardened and darkened, out of the brush. And with the loupe, I was not forced, but was certainly compelled, to take a far closer look at what I'd captured.

These preliminary levels of insect observation are at once the least difficult, most intriguing, and generously rewarding. Why? Because you haven't identified anything yet, but you are now able to base your fly pattern selection on a close look at a natural insect that trout are currently eating. Stick to the prescription of Doug Swisher, coauthor of *Selective Trout:* size, form, and color, in that order of importance. Get them right in your fly, and your catch will jump up, whether you know the insect's Latin name or not.

Next level: Start an insect collection and begin, at some taxonomic level that is not necessarily species, to identify them. I'm not recommending this to you. But I will repeat that anything you learn about trout and the things that live in their world will add to, never subtract from, both your pleasure and your catch.

You'll need some equipment to start a collection: a kick net, a white freezer pan or photo enlargement tray, a pair of tweezers, and some 2- to 3-dram glass vials filled with 80 percent ethyl alcohol. You can make an excellent net yourself with two 3-foot lengths of ¾-inch dowel and a 2-foot-wide by 3-foot-long sheet of fine-mesh fiberglass window screening. Roll the ends of the screen once around each dowel, leaving 2 inches of each dowel exposed at one end to probe into the streambottom and 10 inches exposed at the other end for handles. Staple the screen to the dowel, and you own a fine aquatic insect collecting net.

To collect with it, wade into a riffle, run, flat, pool, or any water type with some current. Open the net downstream from you, and dig the 2 inches of exposed dowel into the bottom so that the screen bows with the current and hugs tight to the bottom. Shuffle your feet in the gravel upstream from the net. Kick over a few stones, and toe into the substrate, dislodging insects. Lift the net up and toward you so that whatever you've captured is held in place by the pressure of the current until the net is out of the water.

Wade to shore and spread the net on the ground. Fill your tray with an inch or two of water and place it next to the net.

Now get down on your knees and begin tweezering trapped insects off the mesh of the net and into the tray. Be gentle to keep from killing the insects before you're able to observe their natural movements in the tray.

It's likely you'll be surprised at the variety you capture. It's also likely that some insect or other will be dominant in your collection. That's the one you want to choose a fly to imitate. It's also the one you want to transfer from the tray to a vial and take home to your tying bench.

You'll collect different types of insects from different environments in the same stream. It's best to take a sample from a riffle, another from a nearby run, to scoop the net through any rooted vegetation, and perhaps to run it up under any undercut banks. Each sample will reveal some insects that overlap with those from other samples, and others that are unique to that environment. For example, you'll find lots of clinger mayflies and some small swimmers in riffles, fewer clingers and more big swimmer nymphs in undercuts.

It's not advisable to rape any stream with your collecting, and it's especially important to limit your samples on delicate spring creek environments or on any water that is heavily waded and fished. Use good judgment. Moderate collecting in a healthy environment will neither deplete insects nor damage the stream-bottom, but don't go around tearing everything up or you'll make yourself unpopular. If you don't wish to preserve specimens for your tying, release them unharmed into the stream. Don't worry about returning them to the exact spot where you found them. Get them back into the water as soon as you've finished with them; they'll find their own way home.

At this stage of your collecting career, your references might as well be angling books, not entomology texts.

Why angling books? Because your goal should be to place what you collect into the framework of what has already been collected and written about by others in fishing terms. Don't try to identify every insect to species. Do try to recognize what you've collected to the most specific taxonomic level possible, on the scale from order to family to genus to species—usually family or genus—and see what patterns have been tied for it and, perhaps more important, what methods have been devised to fish those patterns.

When you begin preserving insects, write when and where you collected your sample, in pencil on white paper, and place this label inside the vial with them. If you fail to do this, you'll end up with a tangle of dead bugs that is no help in untangling your fishing.

I recommend you also begin a type-species collection. By this I mean set aside, in a drawer or on display, one vial of each type of insect that you collect, in taxonomic descent of order, family, genus, and even species in those rare cases where you'll identify it that far down with any degree of assurance. A problem that anglers have always had, one that greatly disturbs professional entomologists, is our overwhelming desire to identify every aquatic insect to species even when we're wrong.

In the end—and the beginning, for that matter—with such an ordered collection, you'll be able to step right to your sample of *Pteronarcys californica* or *Hexagenia limbata* and look it over for your own reference or pull it out to impress your friends. You'll create your own framework for understanding the world of aquatic insects. If your collection is based on a small set of home waters, you'll increase your knowledge of those waters in angling terms and might even make a significant contribution in professional terms. Ordered collections on single bodies of water are rare and valuable.

The final level, and this is where you leave me behind, is the world of microscopes, entomology texts, and exact identification. It's an all-absorbing hobby . . . or an occupation. I've always left identification to species to professionals, having been blessed with the early and great luck to have Rick Hafele as a fishing partner and friend. He's got a master's degree in aquatic entomology, has a job in his field that keeps him constantly on top of changes in taxonomy, and so far has been willing to answer most of my questions.

You can take collecting, observing, and identifying aquatic insects to whatever level suits you. Any level at all will help you, never hurt you. Always keep in mind the twin ends toward which your study is directed: more accurate fly pattern selection and more realistic fly pattern presentation. Those are the main ways in which insect identification will increase your fly-fishing success, at any level.

Bibliography

Bergman, Ray. *Trout.* New York: Crown, 1938.

Berners, Dame Juliana. *Treatyse of Fysshynge with an Angle.* Westminster: 1496.

Borger, Gary. *Nymphing.* Harrisburg, PA: Stackpole Books, 1979.

Gierach, John. *Trout Bum.* Boulder, CO: Pruett, 1986.

Hafele, Rick, and Scott Roederer. *Aquatic Insects and Their Imitations.* Boulder, CO: Johnson Books, 1987.

Hidy, Pete, and James Leisenring. *The Art of Tying the Wet Fly.* New York: E. P. Dutton, 1941.

Hughes, Dave. *Reading the Water.* Harrisburg, PA: Stackpole Books, 1988.

Humphreys, Joe. *Trout Tactics.* Harrisburg, PA: Stackpole Books, 1981.

Judy, John. *Slack Line Strategies for Fly Fishing.* Mechanicsburg, PA: Stackpole Books, 1994.

Krieger, Mel. *The Essence of Fly Casting.* San Francisco: Club Pacific, 1987.

LaFontaine, Gary. *Caddisflies.* New York: Winchester Press, 1981.

Lee, Art. *Fishing Dry Flies for Trout on Rivers and Streams.* New York: Atheneum, 1983.

Leeson, Ted. *Habit of Rivers.* New York: Lyons & Burford, 1994.

McMorris, Bill, and Jo McMorris. *Camp Cooking.* New York: Lyons & Burford, 1988.

Morris, Skip. *The Custom Graphite Fly Rod.* New York: Lyons & Burford, 1989.

Nemes, Sylvester. *The Soft-Hackled Fly.* Chatham, 1975. Reprint. Mechanicsburg, PA: Stackpole Books, 1993.

————. *Soft-Hackled Fly Addict.* Chicago: Author, 1981. Reprint. Mechanicsburg, PA: Stackpole Books, 1993.

Pritt, T. E. *Yorkshire Trout Flies.* London: Samson, Low, Marston, Searle & Rivington, 1886.

Richmond, Scott. *Pocket Ghillie.* West Linn, OR: Four Rivers Press, 1992.

Rosborough, Polly. *Tying and Fishing the Fuzzy Nymphs.* Fourth Edition. Harrisburg, PA: Stackpole Books, 1978.

Schollmeyer, Jim. *Hatch Guide for Western Streams.* Portland, OR: Frank Amato Publications, 1997.

Scott, Jock. *Greased Line Fishing for Atlantic Salmon.* London: Seeley, Service & Co., 1935.

Swisher, Doug, and Carl Richards. *Fly Fishing Strategy.* New York: Lyons Press, 1987.

Swisher, Doug, and Carl Richards. *Selective Trout.* Reprint. New York: Lyons Press, 1987.

Stewart, W. C. *The Practical Angler.* London: Adam & Charles Black, 1857.

Tolstoy, Leo. *The Cossacks and the Raid.* New York: Signet Classics Edition, 1961.

Index

About the Author

Dave Hughes is editor of *Flyfishing & Tying Journal* and a contributing editor to *Field & Stream*. His twenty-five books include *Trout Flies* and *Western Hatches,* coauthored with Rick Hafele.

He lives in Portland, Oregon, with his wife and daughter.